Higher Education As Ignorance

The Contempt of Mexicans in the American Educational System

Julián Segura Camacho

Hamilton Books
A member of
The Rowman & Littlefield Publishing Group
Lanham • Boulder • New York • Toronto • Plymouth, UK

LC 2683.6
.S44
2008
c.3

Copyright © 2008 by
Hamilton Books
4501 Forbes Boulevard
Suite 200
Lanham, Maryland 20706
Hamilton Books Acquisitions Department (301) 459-3366

Estover Road
Plymouth PL6 7PY
United Kingdom

All rights reserved
Printed in the United States of America
British Library Cataloging in Publication Information Available

Library of Congress Control Number: 2008923449
ISBN-13: 978-0-7618-4026-8 (paperback : alk. paper)
ISBN-10: 0-7618-4026-5 (paperback : alk. paper)

∞™ The paper used in this publication meets the minimum
requirements of American National Standard for Information
Sciences—Permanence of Paper for Printed Library Materials,
ANSI Z39.48—1992

Dedicated to:

Monica Segura Camacho,
Mi Madrecita y Sagrado Corazon

Teresa Aartman Muela,
Mi Suegra; My Second Mother As My Mother Says

This is to acknowledge those of us who were not able to complete a college degree but who carry more Mexican American life knowledge than any PhD:

In Your Honor I have written this!

#26.00

THECB

7/26/10

Contempt:

An intense feeling of disrespect and dislike. It is similar to hate, but implies feelings of superiority. A person who has contempt for another individual looks down on that person. The recipient of contempt is deemed unworthy, beneath consideration. Contempt may be related to feelings of disgust and bitterness.

The old adage, "familiarity breeds contempt" means that we get sick of people and places that we see every day. In fact, however, familiarity generally produces attraction. This is documented as the mere exposure effect in psychology.

In a legal sense, contempt means disrespect for the authority of the court. A contempt of court charge may be brought against those who are unruly or disobedient.

From Wikipedia, the free encyclopedia
February 20, 2007

Contents

Introduction: Modern Missions

The endless debate about educational achievement, advancement, success, and failure takes place on a weekly basis in societal circles. In the paradigmatic discussion of 21st century education, the bluff of technological knowledge or the acquisition of English and excellent writing skills, a comparative and wicked analysis is made between groups in the US.

In California, Los Angeles County to be exact, Mexicans are the most insulted and scorned group that never seems to progress.

As an American product of Mexican people, a product socialized north of the great Mexican divide, I have lived this experience of insult and contempt as I was educated. As a part time professor, it continues. My personal experiences are case studies in some of education's greatest debates: being Mexican or American; learning English ONLY; standardize testing; 50% dropout rates at Los Angeles Unified School District; the high failure rate of the high school exit examination; 10% of Mexican Americans who attend community college transfer; only 10–15% graduate from a 4-year institution; the elimination of basic skills courses at the California State University system; intentional failing of Mexicans by the basic skills examination (CBEST) for k–12 instruction; low scores on the SAT; low admission rates to college as freshmen; low number of professionals in medicine or law; and of course, the view that Mexican culture and Mexican Spanish is a hindrance to success in education. The reasons are endless and above all without merit.

In my family, we have lived it all. Although my parents encouraged education, four out of my five brothers failed grades in the 1970–80s by these "professionals" in the elementary schools. Alberto was failed in the 3rd grade—how does that happen at age 8, Ricardo in 4th or 5th grade, David in 3rd grade (and then he went on to spent many years in a special educational facility only to be placed in his appropriate age group in 8th grade) and Jorge failed 3rd grade. How can a system fail four out of five siblings in one household? Even my mother wondered what the hell was happening, not enough tutoring, not enough attention; she attended every meeting she was summoned to and tried to answer the useless questions.

How could we have failed if we spoke two languages and well?

Even my niece in Calexico has been placed in continuation high school. Yet, she continues to work to complete her courses. Still from these high failures rates, all of my family members graduated from high school even three at age 19—we never gave up. The high school diploma was mandatory even if not valued in today's economy.

I did not fare much better than my brothers. I had a 590 SAT score and a 600 graduate aptitude score (GRE), which were both considered failing scores. Furthermore, I had to endure three different White college professors from El Camino College to UCLA who told me that I could not write that I was not graduate school material. The UCLA professor (John Freidman) was an immigrant from Germany who learned English as a second language. How could a second language learner tell a US born citizen that my writing was not suited for graduate school? And yet he could. To this day, I have not passed that famous teaching examination (CBEST) because I need five more points in math. Plus, I refuse to re-take the GRE because I feel they are merely testing to "prove" I am unintelligent.

And yet, the Camacho—Guerrero families are warriors as our maternal grandmother's last name states. We fight, amongst each other and anybody who crosses our paths. We fight for survival, and educational racism did not hold us back. Three of us have completed our college degrees: David from Oklahoma State University, Ricardo from California State University-Northridge, and me from USC and UCLA. My other two brothers have completed at least 30 units at the community college, while becoming part of a group trapped at the community college—an educational facility that only worries about enrollment but not completion much less graduation rates.

Indeed, high failure rates of Mexican American students guarantee a student body population for those White faculty, their steady jobs, and their lavish benefits.

What truly emerges is that fact that American schools are nothing more than Modern Missions based on the Catholic Missionization of Northern Mexican people also called Indians. How can people with a culture be instructed by people with no culture? The average White is not bilingual and does not carry ancestral Mexican Apache knowledge of cuisine, architecture, music, geography, agriculture or a deeper comprehension of the spirit world. How are they rooted in the soil of California? Where is their footing?

Today's missions—schools—are primarily composed of White people. Even in the heart of the barrios, the majority are White and never more than 25% Mexicans. The teacher is generally White, monolingual in English (English only). Whereas, the average Chicano student is bilingual and has more linguistic knowledge than his teacher because he uses both sides of his brain to think. But the monolingual person is more intelligent, right?

Obviously, the curriculum is English driven and the system spends millions of dollars to change the desert culture of California from Mexican to Anglo. The other subjects follow suit: all instruction in English and all knowledge reinforces Western European superiority.

The arrogant "we know better" curriculum is driven by a Superintendent who is not an educator but more of a warden. The recent school lockdowns prove that. Even if there are Mexican teachers or principals, they are just there to enforce a script, a White script handed to them, whether they are truly conscious of it or not. If they were, they probably would not be teaching. However, there are not that many career choices for Chicano college graduates. Simultaneously, I know many want to change the failure of American schoolings because they too lived it. But they are handed a school-board approved script that many cannot move away from. All they are supposed to do is read it. How is that education?

Even the word principal means more of laying down the rules with a ruler than actual centers of knowledge. No high school is truly known to be a center of knowledge but more a place to perfect following rules. If it was not for the socializing teens enjoy from their fellow students, the graduation rates would even be lower. The beautiful girl next to you is more appealing than Steinbeck or Fitzgerald. Her scent suffices.

This book is a Mexican American counter culture to the hatred created by the educational system that kills the culture brought into the classroom and replaces it with ignorance. The more education Mexicans have, the more Anglo they tend to be and vice versa, the less American education Mexicans have, the more Mexican they remain. Ultimately, the workplace does not really care for education, for they can teach you what they want you to know.

Concurrently, everything I have explained does not mean that I do not want to learn or be knowledgeable. I completed college as a duty, yet I have done more reading on my own and without being dictated what to read or write. I have written four books with those low SAT and GRE scores, and I have been learning how to play the guitar without Whiteness interrupting. I love my own learning process because I write from my maternal Apache Mexican perspective not from some White professor who cannot even pronounce my name correctly.

Many thanks to the following people:
  Mi esposa Joanna for inspiring and hearing me out!
  Mis hermanos: Elizabeth, Mario Alberto, Ricardo, David y Jorge.
  Mi tia Guadalupe Delgadillo;
  Antonio, Tony and Guadalupe Perez in Mexicali, B.C.
  Marco Antonio Ramos en Oakland
  Ruben Lopez en East Los Angeles
  John Morales of Mission College, Jose Mungaray for reading the early
chapters, Rosalinda Moctezuma for important Chicano dialogues, Norma
Montoya for the beautiful painting of "Unwanted and Not Included",
Maulana Karenga and John Caldwell who defended me once when nobody
else would, Ramiro Sandoval and the staff en el Greenleaf Café en el Rancho
Paso de Bartolo, some call Whittier.
  A special special mil gracias to Joanne Aartman for the picture book cover
and the great editing.
  To Usen; the Cucapah y el Este de Los Angeles: East LA.
  Chiro Chido Chilo!

Chapter One

White Teachers As Mothers

The foundation of Mexican people is laid by our mothers nuestras madrecitas; jefas; ama; mi existencia; la mujer quien me dio vida. The first and most obvious rationale is that our mother's carried us for nine months and because she painfully labored in the birthing of us as an independent life form, we as her offspring will forever be indebted to her. Until death and even after death.

The philosophy of the mother revolves around the notion that one is truly a miracle, for no explanation is provided to why one is born. In the most simplistic and humorous analysis, the Tecate and Tequila did wonders to braven our fathers to approximate himself to this woman, most likely at a Club or un baile as they would say. The alcohol created visions of beauty and hormones drove the rest.

To be born of an urge, as a flash in the universe is mystical and without comprehension. In those nine months that future mother nurtures through her own mouth and diet based on the exquisite cocina Mexicana, an inseparable bond is developed as the growth of the fetus occurs. Only a mother who has lived through this experience can discern this eternal link for this second life to cultivate into a futuristic independent life, which nonetheless will depend on the mother for at least another twenty years.

In time, the offspring's is dependence will become independent through years of daily care and daily nourishment which will mean continuously being lead throughout most of the stages of life that the mother can be part of.

Mexican philosophy values this channel of birth religiously. This I have seen in multiple forms. First, through my parents in my reverence and obedience towards them. Only my ama and apa Alberta and Matiaz could stop my mother Monica from disciplining us (I have five other siblings). I saw that as a child and realized that my apa Matiaz had not just influence but the moral power to halt chanclazos. As children, we needed chingazos, so we would learn. We did get spanked when we were being potty-trained and still peed or nos cagamos. My apa had the power to calm my mother down and he would take charge. He would protect us from my mother and she would listen. It was an incredible sight to view; my mother took orders without question from her father. And he bathed us with a wet rag when we cried because we did not want a baño. It was an inferior baño, but he did not want to see us cry. My mother would later laugh at his baños. My ama Alberta could do the same and discipline us too, but she rarely did. My brothers usually referred to her belt as her 30-30 trienta trienta.

My mother revered her mother as a saint. My ama was a rancho woman in the Imperial Valley, in Mexicali. When my third brother Ricardo was born, he was named through her because she asked my mother if she would name him based on the day she was born in 1924. Her saint day was Ricarda, el dia de su santo. When I found this out after mi ama Alberta died in 2004, I learned then that a great reverence for that elder mother was simple and beyond this universe.

As I helped bury my elder mother, we did not refer to her as abuela grand-mother but as mother—ama in Apachis. I stared at my mother in the distance and saw this anger of pain in my mother. I could not console her. She was just irate at life with her livid face and there learned about Mexican philosophy. In this life, there is only one mother. *One solely has a mother, she is your life.* If you do not have a mother, you have no life, and at the moment, I buried my mother's life and the mother of five tios y tias and thirty grandchildren, half were not hers but through kinship and yet they were there to say goodbye. Part of us died there too.

My father revered his mother too. Although he passed away several years ago, as an adult today, I can grasp their bond through my own mother. My father Julian who died in 1980 had a union with Luz that I saw segments of. As the eldest son, I was awarded a kind of special privilege through mi mami (she instructed us to refer to her as mama grande because she was the mother of my father). I knew my father was extraordinary through her smile to me. She babied me in a way that made others jealous including my father's siblings. Mami would make me what I wanted *y me chiquiaba; to be mijoed.* She would cook, talk to me as an adult, and protected me. And Luz was a warrior of seasonal farming in between Salinas and El Centro; she was a homeowner, a coyote, a provider, an instigator and a woman who lost a son to the unknown of a heart aneurysm.

My mother and she have clashed all my life because my father was Luz's mijo. My mother has always warned me about her and yet always encouraged me to visit her in the Imperial Valley. I rode with her in the hearst as we delivered my father to nuestra tierra, mother earth. I saw a mother's pain for her dead son that even I did not comprehend. She sat stoically, faced forward as her son enjoyed his final drive through the dusty streets of his weekend home in Mexicali. I could not console her, she could not weep anymore, she would wait eternally for her offspring. To bury her son was her cross to carry; a permanent rupture had taken place, for she would never see her son again. The linkage between she and I was now dead. She forever cries for Julian Padilla Camacho, more than me Julian Segura Camacho, for my mother is still alive. And yet I dread the day when I must return my mother to earth, for I will have lost my reason for being. For me, mothers are gods. That is why when they fail, the pain is that much more profound and hurtful.

Hence if we worship them philosophically, we also complement the worship through song. Mexicans sing to their mothers. The most famous Mexican songs: Tres coronas pa mi madre; Amor eterno; Ni por mil puñados de oro; La llorona y others. We celebrate Mother's Day on May 10th and the Anglo Mother's Day simply to recognize our mothers on two days not just once. All because she gave us life through her pleasure.

And from day one of our life outside of our mother, she does daily and monotonous duties for us: feeds us through pecho or tetera; clothes us; bath us; wipes the caca off of us; holds us when we cry and I cried a lot. In the first picture my mother and me after my birth in El Centro, California, in the black and white, she looks down at me with a smile

My mother and I bonded; she fed me great Mexican Apache food. She made tortillas de harina, huevos con papas, frijoles; she spoiled me by giving me a bottle and would send me to hide under the covers so my father would not see me with a chupon in my mouth. I had to get off the tetera; me tenia que ser hombre. And he was right, I had to become a man and my mother gradually walked me to manhood first through childhood.

Mi mama taught me to walk; bathe which I did not like; watch the news; imagine; express myself; clean; sing; protect myself by running; and permitting me to speak endless cycles of words while my father provided the means to do so. Monica taught me my first language—Mexican from California. She dressed me and took me to beach and the rancho in Inglewood at my adopted grandparent's home. Gus and Kika Magaña were my Mexican padrinos known as Nino and Nina—Apache words for kinship and we were never separated from them until death.

My mother even brought a brother into my life, so I would not be alone. From the moment Alberto arrived in 1972 from the Inglewood Hospital, I wanted to play with him so much that I almost smothered him with a pillow. My mother taught me to be gentile and careful. He was an infant; I was a growing child. She later taught me how to bathe my youngest brother when I was ten. She was always teaching life.

She read the newspaper and I listened. She watched the news and I sat with her. I had to know what was going on in the world. I still watch the news. My father would tell us, es puro chisme; pure gossip. I learned to play with toys and color because she showed me. I colored all the time, broke apart Tonka trucks and listened to rancheras on a daily basis when LPs were the norm. She would buy them on credit in Inglewood, my childhood rancho that died years ago.

This cycle of learning was not new. My mother had learned many important child development skills and life skills through her mother. My ama Alberta had taught my ama Monica how to cook from scratch—Mexican culinary. This meant she had to have knowledge of vegetables, meats, fruits, spices, measurements, how to mix masa and roll tortillas out. Qui'vo! Monica even learned how to milk a cow and ride horses from her father.

She learned how to sew by hand and later by using a foot peddle Sears sewing machine. Monica until this day knows how to make her own clothing. A fashion designer a la rancho style which includes crocheting, scarves and blanket making. She learned this through her master teacher: her mother.

Another important skill was learned through the knowledge of plants both for medicine and for brujeria power. Each plant and flower contains healer curative powers for the body and soul that can only be transmitted from mother to daughter within Mexican Apache culture (el mercado de brujeria en el DF is called el mercado Sonora). Mexicali is in the western Sonoran desert of Califas divided by the mother snake called el Rio Colorado. One had to be born into this and transmitted through blood. The culture reinforced the positiveness of this ritual because most ranchos were self sustaining. Even the doctors resorted to curative powers of herbs such as manzanilla to cure irritated eyes; te de limon that cures stomach ailments. My mother's pharmacy is in the backyard in the chiles, savilas, nopales, hierba buenas and rudas. I would pick ruda for my mother as a child in Inglewood.

In essence, my mother's mother was a combination of three graduate schools in one: culinary, home economics, pharmacy. The culture taught her lifelong skills that she could always build upon if given an opportunity. The US side would only want her labor and not her knowledge.

By the time I was born, in the Imperial Valley but on the US side, the traditional society my mother was born into fifteen miles south was dying on the US side. My father and his mother labored as factory workers in the fields as lechugeros or tomato packers. Yes, my father's occupation at the time of my birth was stated on my birth certificate

as Tomato Packer and Caucasian. The US Government began lying to me at birth. My father was a second generation Apache Mexican American migrant farm worker. His best skills were to drive his family up and down 1,000 miles of California and to sustain long hours of back-breaking stoop labor.

Still he was a macho about it. His mother taught him what he needed to learn, and although he went to school here in the US, the economy and their poverty forced him to be a junior high dropout. My father was part of child labor in the US, forced to work to survive. He worked to provide fruit and vegetables for his Anglo counterparts. However, he learned. He was schooled at the university of the streets and fields.

After a few years of school with my mother, it came time for me to enter kindergarten. At this young age, I heard the great expectations of my parents, "You need to study hard to succeed in life." I did not fully grasp their saying of course. As I prepared to attend Oak Street Elementary, there was a feeling of great enthusiasm. Both of my parents were educated as was normal in Mexicali which was elementary completion. That education was about ideals and notions such as reading and symbols, but Mexicans were oral so memory served more of an important tool than actual reading. Memorization through oral stories was more vital than reading and telling somebody's story. They had their own stories to tell from two generations back. Even Joaquin Murrieta was part of the folklore because according to them just to the west from the rancho at the beautiful cerro del centinela was where Joaquin had hidden some of the gold during the Gold Rush era. A mere 150 years prior.

What my parents did not know and many do not is the policy of removing children from the home was mandatory so Missionization could occur. Contrary to popular belief, Mexicans believe highly in public education. They did not hesitate to send children to schools because they believe that their children need to succeed in life.

Little did they know that the system would use (and continues to use) White women as surrogates mothers. Elementary school in Mexicali, Baja California is only four hours. The child spends enough time away from the mother but not too long. A child eats at his home with his mother, the best cocinera in the world and most Mexican mothers were exceptional. Ask any Mexican and he will tell you that his mother was the best chef. The Mexican educational system very much reinforces the notion of imbedding national symbols but not by severing the child from the mother. They accept the fact the mother would continue her cultural education and that matters as equally or even more than schooling.

In the American elementary schools, especially from first grade on, the child is spending close to seven hours away. He is literally taken from the home for close to the standard 8 hour work day. The American rational here is more akin to expanding conquest. Consequently, because Mexicans are native people to California, White domination had to be rooted out for many hours and years. According to Edward Spicer in his book *Cycles of Conquest*, the Anglos implemented and regulated work hours and compulsory education from the early beginning of their conquest of Northern Mexico. Whites schools are the modern missions, reprogramming had to take place to kill the culture, to change the culture to make one believe in White symbols, to instill a new language on Aztlan. English would now be the language of the desert, of Northern Mexico.

In order to obtain this objective, children had to be removed from the parent as had been done in the Midwest through Indian schools. The Americans severed the umbilical cord between the mother and the child. They did this through new mothers.

White female teachers are used as the new mothers. When feminists argue that White women were only allowed to be teachers as professionals in the 1950's and 1960's, what they fail to realize is that: in California, they were utilized as soldiers for the empire. The empire had achieved military victory, but the real conquest was in the mind and spirit of the new generations that were tied to a Mexican mother, who was linked to Mother Earth. Because the Mexican mother was never severed from Mother Earth, the culture would maintain itself intact even if aliens or armies arrived. I was told as a child by family friends, older White men who were World War I veterans, that we Mexicans were the true Californians not them. The Califorences!

These comments by White men reinforced what my grandfather and mother had always educated me about: we were California Mexicans, we were not immigrants even if we were born on the other side of the border, and it was all Califas. Baja California; southern California. California is not an Anglo word, it is Mexican.

Still, this historical geographical linkage had to be erased through genocidal education, and White women were the devils hired to do so. They were given access to college to reach out to Mexican children throughout California with a check. The system further comprehended this bond between the Mexican mother and Mexican child, so they implemented the new White mother in kindergarten through four hour sessions. And to reinforce the new mother figure, for us kindergarten children, they utilized two mothers. Two White mothers reinforced enough attention to make us Mexican children feel safe.

Our mothers agreed to this chicanery because they understood that there were new rules and were more petrified of their children having to do manual slave labor as they did. The hope was in the sons or daughters that they would learn enough to survive from using their cerebral. No education guaranteed field or factory work at low pay; schooling created the allusion of hope. There were no choices. For our jefas, it was a difficult situation; afterall, what normal mother wants her children to be away from her. Playing with other children or facilities that were better than most parks provided a sense of hope, but those White teachers with their history of Whiteness and anti

Mexican-ness would diabolically attack the Mexican spirit consciously or not.

It is Anglo society that replaces the Mexican mother with a White teacher mother. My mother had taught me enough, I could speak in Mexican Spanish and knew enough English to survive. My father was Mexican American, my Nina Kika spoke to me in both languages, my uncles and tias were all bilingual. I knew two languages by the age of five. How much more literate did I need to be? None of my White teachers knew Mexican Spanish. How literate were they and they lived in Los Angeles? That to me is akin to living in New York and not knowing English.

The new White teacher mothers began what Zac de la Rocha explains in his powerful song, "Know Your Enemy," to teach us to fight. Mispronunciation of names: these White teachers mispronounced my name and created my identity in English. I never went by Jul-ee-an; it was always Huli-an in Mexican. These white teacher mothers were already inflicting cultural clashes from kindergarten. Moreover, I had my own identity issue because my father was Julián too. I was Juliancito. In the Camacho clan, I was Juliancito almost up to age 33. I went through high school with my name being annunciated in English until I had enough confidence to correct my college instructors. Say my name in Mexican, con una chingada!

Interestingly, the teachers always made sure I pronounced their names correctly in English. I spoke with my beautiful Mexican accent, and they would stop to correct my pronunciation of their names in their language. I had to get it right. My assimilation was taking hold from age five, almost instantly.

Then came the Ingles. Ingles took hold. Ingles was so dominant that I felt I was in between two countries, one in the classroom and one out on the street. I state the street because I grew up not only speaking Mexican in the household but throughout all of Inglewood. My Mexicanization was not confined to a house. Our neighbors spoke Mexican but depending on their origin, their accents were different; the local carniceria, the lavanderia, the relatives, all spoke Nahualt. There were Blacks and Whites, but we only spoke to them on rare occasions unless they were White trash hippies or neighborhood Blacks. The hippie neighbor was coined Zapata by my tio, and my parents spoke to her in Ingles when needed.

Yet in that classroom, I felt the different country through those White women. My name was different with them and so was the usage of English only. These White teacher mothers did not look or have names like my mother. I used to wonder what it would be like to have a teacher who looks like you and talks like you. In my K-8 years of Angloization, I only had one teacher who was Mexicano, Mr. Fuentes at Crozier Junior High School in 7th grade. I really enjoyed it and felt I could connect with him, but half of the time he was yelling his head off at the obnoxious White and Black students who misbehaved intentionally. To hear him decir chingaderas at those students was incredible because that is how I would hear those emotions played out in my upbringing.

He would say enough profanity in between his breath so we Mexicans could hear him but I could not fault him. Those White and Black students disrupted our bond with him too. I would intentionally sit in the front along with other Mexican students. We longed for someone like him only to be brought back to other White or Black female teachers. It was for one semester only. In high school I had a Casillas teacher, but he was afraid to be Mexican and it showed.

Beyond Mr. Fuentes and the lost Chicano, White women were our teachers. Returning to elementary school, those White women reinforced their Americanization into us. English became the norm with a smile and we bonded with them whether we liked it nor not. There was no linkage between the household and the school.

Still regardless of the teacher, once in the classroom, I would want to bond with my teacher because I saw her for many hours. And yet they pushed English into us as a suppository. The "he needs reading practice" criticism. Then I began learning English from a family friend, a teenager from Inglewood High School. Alfonso was neither Black nor White, but a Mexican American, we were there too. Alfonso Coronado taught me to annunciate.

The White American devil was cruel, so my taste buds taught me. We were removed early and they enticed us with breakfast and lunch. Now no normal Mexican child would want to surrender his papas con huevos y tortillas o chorizo, yet we had to. Those peanut butter crackers plastered my teeth so much that I believe much of my dental cavities stemmed from the high sugar and not being able to rinse my mouths thoroughly. The little cartons of milk were never enough. There I learned my first lessons of American capitalism, exchange for something else. It was never enough. At home, I could drink all the milk I wanted.

Lunch was just as disastrous and tasteless. Fuckin' corndogs? I used to eat those when my mother was working as a last resort to kill hunger until she arrived home. A tortilla with wienie would never be lunch. My mother frightened us with the lumbrice (tapeworm) story, eating wienies would give us maggots in our stomachs. Sometimes I wonder if this is how I was sterilized by American society. Because my father had seeded five males before age 29 in Los Angeles and my mother made deep fried tacos and pollo frito, how could school food be better?

I just followed orders from my parents to study hard. I enjoyed my fellow classmates, but schooling did not connect with my household. Ultimately, these teachers were distant from us too so I never really knew much about my instructor.

Then came third grade. My third grade teacher used corporal punishment on us. Mrs. Parker was a pack rack who smacked open hands on all of us. Most of us were Mexican kids with some Blacks and Whites. She hit them too.

I was given a chingazo on my back and it hurt. Enough people complained and she was replaced. I do not know why I did not inform my mother, I was not confident to do so. I think I was afraid to challenge the teacher, she held the power. My mother attended school functions, but for some reason, I was scared maybe in the same way children are afraid of priests or authority figures. Would I run to my mother all the time? I do not have an answer. But the administration knew of this problem teacher, so she was retired to our relief (and no doubt paid her well deserved pension) and a new one was hired.

The new teacher Draher or Draper turned out to be another bitch but at least not with her fist. I am notorious for being late to everything. In those days, I was on time, and on her first day, I arrived to class early and walked in eager to meet her and her approval. I walked in, said hello and the bitch yelled at me: "Go outside and get in line." Here I was full of enthusiasm, I arrived early and she saluted me with a mean scream. I felt like shit. I learned then and there that following orders and getting in line was more important than showing up early to class. I cannot tell you why I am late now, but maybe I learned then that taking orders mattered more to them than feeling safe with our teachers. I went through the motions and moved on to fourth grade. More English, math and learning how to write in fancy lettering. I never listened to rancheras in school the way I did at home. They were two continents apart, a mere eight blocks.

My fourth grade teacher was a Cuban woman. Many people believe Cubans and Mexicans are the same. I instantly realized that her name might have been Rivero, but we looked different and spoke different. Truth of the matter, Mexicans and Cubans in Los Angeles do not like each other, just as Puerto Ricans and Cubans do not like each other. Why? Cubans believe they are better than us, and in those years, Rivero proved that Cubans could do better than us. Never in my wildest dream, could I imagine a Mexican as a teacher. Rivero was an immigrant, a special refugee who was a college graduate all because of Fidel, Fidelito. I never even believed that my mother could be a teacher. That was how I was made to feel about her. The distance now of four years moved me away from the early linkages with my mother. My mother encouraged me to do my homework, but there was a distance especially when I had English assignments. I was on my own.

Rivero saw this and paid some extra attention, but she was interested in something else. Saving us Apache heathens from White people's religion whatever that was. After the first parent conference that my mother attended, she talked to seven of our parents, only to Mexicans and asked them if they were interested in making our Holy Communion. All our parents agreed I believe because most Mexicans are Catolicos, not Catholics. Catolicismo meant Mexican rituals. Next thing I knew, we spent five or six months going to her mother's house in Inglewood learning our padre nuestros santoficado sea tu nombre. It was our little secret and we kept it hidden. We learned Rivero was a former monja en Cuba, oye chico and now was her opportunity to convert Mexican Catolicos to Catolicismo. I learned later that I was part of the first group of children to have done our communion in Spanish at St. John's Chrysostom where I had been baptized ten years earlier.

Two years later, I learned why her missionization was important. My sixth grade teacher was Mrs. Rosenthal and she was not the only one who happened to be Jewish. Rosenthal and Ms. Burris practiced Judaism in class by having us learn about Jewish religion, the menorra, the star and the lighting of the candles. Rivero wanted to make sure we were not influenced by their paganism. Oddly enough, Rivero went underground for our Catolicismo but the Jews could openly instill their religious values. I learned how to sing, "O Hannukkah, O Hannukkah, come light the menorah," but I could not sing ranchera songs by Vicente Fernandez that my mother played for me at home. I'm glad I was taught Catolicismo in español with a little Santeria and Chango. Come on, Cubans are African in origin. I would rather be African than White Jewish in spirit, plus la San Juan could be made Mexican whereas Judaism could not. Catolicismo adapted to Mexicanism, Judaism did not.

Hence, White women were changing us through their role as a mother figure, a new language, American symbols, and even a newer type of White religion. My friend Ruben Lopez recently mentioned that his seven-year-old son was using vocabulary he did not comprehend until his roommate Jose Reyes, realized they were Jewish terms he had learned from his film and literature interest as a film major graduate from San Francisco State University. Ruben was livid about this: religion instead of the basics. Judaism is not about the basics.

My sixth grade teacher with her voluptuous breasts spent much time showing us Martin Luther King footage but made no connections to us Mexicans who made up more than half of the students. By this time, I was fluent in English and Mexican Spanish had become secondary. Ahora realmente hablaba como pocho. White schooling had Anglicized me, but my mother kept me grounded. I could never deny I was Mexican because she reinforced me through food, conversation, family and friends and most importantly those beautiful summer excursions to el valle Imperial. I loved visiting Mexicali in the summer time. Con dos semanas en Mexicali perdiamos el acento en ingles. Oddly enough, the local owner of the market called Seferino's was a Chicano from Long Beach. On the visits to the mercado, he would practice English with me. I switched in between ingles y español in an instant. The other Mexicans hated when we spoke English, so I was conscious not to speak it, I was in Mexico. English was the language of the Anglos not of the Mexicans, I was Mexican even if born on the other side.

Fortunately, my mother reinforced study, and we never lost our Mexican-ness. How would we become White if we could not and my Nino was rein-forcing his Michoacan Mexican in us. Mi Nino was the Chicano Patron Saint who already had a record of Mexicanizing other brown gringos.

School became a duty but not my culture. My mother continued teaching her notions of what I should learn as a male. I learned how to clean and to cocinar a little. The White teacher mothers could never assimilate one fact: that my mother was still a brown Mexican woman who I still worshipped and would continue to guide me and teach me into adulthood even when I doubted her intellect. These White teacher mother devils attempted to instill in me that my mother was not smart, but my jefa always proved them wrong all the while making sure I learned English for survival skills only.

The Anglo missions completed their fiend deeds. In many ways, their mis-sion was accomplished: I speak, read and write English. There are many Mex-ican words even after years of learning Mexican literacy that I find myself asking my mother to define for my comprehension. I speak the White Anglo language with a Mexican American accent but Anglo I have not and refuse to become.

Yet, as I have gotten older and wiser, I have realized that importance of my native soul madre earth. These surrogate mothers were just that—proxy, tem-porary, substitute, stand in but I refuse to be brainwashed. As a matter of fact, I hate them and even then I sensed a wrong. As I would walk home and see how some of the Mexican females worshipping those White women by walk-ing them to their cars, I realized I was disgusted by such reverence. I just wanted to go home and be with my mother.

Chapter Two

The Gag of English in California

English is Cultural Genocide for Mexicans in the US.

Julian Segura Camacho
Unwanted and Not Included:
The Saga of Mexican People In The US

Because Ingles was forced upon me as a suppository with no lubrication, *nos la metieron doblada y cuadrada*, an analysis of this on-going cultural rape must be comprehended within the context of children and adults. Is English a justifiable language in Northern Mexico? The lands were the Americans are attempting to redefine themselves as Western people in Mexico.

My whole life I have lived with this battle. I do not know what it is like to live in the part of Mexico were only Nahuatl Spanish is the norm and there is no outside influence from English. At one level, I live psychotic episodes of one spirit spearing another over this issue.

I have lived through interpreting sessions as a child, legislative impositions of English Only, monotonous English writing courses from high school to college and being told by Australian and German immigrant college professors at UCLA that I did not know how to write but they spoke with an accent and I was born in the US. Figure that one out.

I always enjoyed reading because my father and mother did too: from Alarma magazine to the Hollywood Park race track program to La Opinion to fotonovelas and other newspapers. Simultaneously, I attended many library functions at the Inglewood Public Library along Manchester Blvd near La Brea. I enjoyed the autobiographies of Black athletes and wondered why they seemed to have the sympathy story and progress. I knew about OJ Simpson from his biography not television, I was too young to have seen him play. And yet by junior high school, I stopped reading school books.

There was a shift from the enjoyment of reading to grammar and the mathematical construct of the language. I felt I was learning math formulas in grammar versus actually reading. When I attended a second junior high school in Riverside, the White lady was no more that mother figure I mentioned before, she was a Marine Sergeant. She taught through fear at Chemawe Middle School. She was brutal, the kind of tough love my mother had us use to by now. Chingazos were our disciplinary philosophy, because by 1982 there were five of us, all machos. I comprehended this White women's approach and I somewhat liked her teaching style.

Once I learned her grammar approaches I was tranquil with her, but we never really read. We were driven by commands from class to class, bell to bell, lecture to lecture. But we did not really read. Then, we moved back to Inglewood and I attended Felton Junior High School were 90% of the students were Mexicans and English-imposed colonial curriculum was the norm. They exercised such paradigm by making us sit in two hour English grammar courses that was more based on work, work, work versus instruction.

At the Riverside school, there were more Whites and the curriculum was not structured through a forceful mandate. The grammar class with the sergeant was only 50 minutes and I feel I learned more with her than with two hours of busy work. The Felton wig wearing teacher was in the cross of aging and becoming old who had not come to that realization yet. We did not read stories nor biographies the way I had done so on my own at the Inglewood library.

I entered high school turned off from English and was placed in another grammar class with the below average White trash students and us Mexicans from Lennox. By the time I was suppose to read, I had lost all interest. I went through high school not really reading in their English courses. I had to take American Literature if that can exist and the college education books of *Catcher in the Rye* and *Lord of the Flies* but was not impressed nor enamored. I tried with *Catcher in the Rye* because I could relate to the depression and the gloomy outlook that I felt but lost interest and put it down. I hated *The Grapes of Wrath*, it was only about White People. Everything was solely about White People. It was my duty and I cut corners and did the minimum to survive.

I went through high school not reading a Shakespeare story and I am very proud of that. I still will not read any of those sterile Anglo books.

I could also tell we were segregated by residency so all the children were clustered by the neighborhoods one came from based on the junior high school. I was later told I was fortunate to have enrolled in a college English course because I was on the right above ESL program. English classes for the non-college student! I was able to do so because I was involved with a boys school club, and the advisor was the counselor so he granted my request change.

Nonetheless, my reading did not cease. I always read the newspaper and many words I did not comprehend, I looked it up in the dictionary or assumed I understood within the context of the story. This I was religious about. I did glance some of my social science texts, but reading those books never inspired me. They have no emotion, they are technical books. But I did my duty.

As I entered the community college system, testing was already an obstacle. We were forced to take placement tests and I qualified the second time around for the college transfer course. I had rationalized that I was not going to waste my time on English courses that were not transferable. Mexican español was all but dead except for this little excursion I took with a family to Monterrey and Torreon in Mexico. I was culturally changed and I wanted to better my pocho Spanish. And I did.

Mexican nationals can be very cruel if one mispronounces words. We are judged as too American and English was viewed in us as lowering ourselves. On the spot and in front of anybody they correct you. It almost seems they are taking out their anti-American sentiments on us because even I do it with people today as adults. Their question of why don't you speak proper Spanish is lost in their lack of comprehension in the American educational system, English gags Mexicanism. In the accumulated process of learning Ingles we slowly but not entirely lose Mexican Spanish. It almost seems that my knowledge of Nahuatl Spanish ended at age five, at the moment that I entered elementary school.

Bilingual education was non-existent, and because I was not an arrival from el otro lado de Mexico, ESL was not part of my discourse. In addition, I do not know if my school district had bilingual education the way east side schools might have had. I lived in a very small barrio that was interracially mixed with Blacks and Whites, they were English speaking already. I do not ever remember not speaking English, it seems I always spoke both. The English as a Second Language program was set apart, and the students that attended were looked down upon but not as much as maybe in high school. In my elementary years, it seemed the ESL students went to another session for a class and then returned. They were not permanently separated the way they were in high school. In high school they were bungalowed or set apart similar to mechanics or woodshop. Mispronouncing Mexican words was brutal, so I learned quickly to pronounce them correctly and it was soothing on the soul. Not by the classroom but through conversation, asking and songs.

The mandatory requirement of English at El Camino College to me was about graduation. I wanted to get it over with and move on, more of a duty but I realized that the terror of six or seven essays weighed on me. I read the stories; I struggled to write the essays doing all nighters on a typewriter my mother purchased for me. The forever guidance she was and my typing skills in the long run proved to be the most important course I ever took in k–12 apart from the sexual educational sessions. I remember neither connecting or enjoying the stories, I remember looking at the back of the book and seeing the pictures of the writers. I only saw White Albinos except for some writer named Gabriel Garcia Marquez. The instructor skipped his story and focused on the *Heart of Darkness*, which I never understood. Maybe he was the darkness.

The instructor complained how I was a terrible writer, I felt he focused on me and I had no ideal he was. Naively I taught he was supposed to be teaching me how to write, he wanted me already to know how to write. In high school we did not write the way he required us to write. In high school, we did summaries but not long essays much less research papers. High school and college seemed to have nothing in common from their writing to even the amount of time spent there. I came to enjoy the freedom of less time in school. The instructor, I slowly despised him, I only wanted the C for transfer, me valia madre su puto ingles. I had completed the six essays they wanted for transfer to a four year institution. Waterworth complained that we did not know how to write, worthless and lazy, he turned out to be. I was more than ever turned away from English, but I had to complete the course. Even in 1987, college faculty were complaining high schoolers did not know how to write, I felt he focused on me after his Lennox comment. I knew he meant Mexicans do not know how to write. I still did not see the connection other than one will write in all their college courses.

The second English course was more relaxed and the instructor loved to hear himself teach. I have to admit, I enjoyed his presence and lecture. He was more like a performer with his goofy tie and Martian eye glasses. He was at least kind and courteous. He worked the class hard on the first essay, eight pages, but all the other essays were short and brief. He employed the old vocabulary listing and I squeaked through with a B. I did better than my first English class but was happy I had passed the courses and would never ever, ever, ever, ever have to enroll in an English class in my life again. And I have not, much less read British or American English stories. I wanted nothing to do with this empire. I enrolled in Spanish courses and learned how to read Spanish, Mexican español.

As I sat in my first Spanish literature course, I realized I did not know how to read in my first language and in a language I knew how to speak. I recognized the words, but I pronounced some of them in English. I knew how to read very little and learned then how to read in Español and yet I wrote my English in español.

I purposely majored in Spanish to be literate but also as a rejection of English. I was going to employ the language I knew I had grown up with until I came across Castellian, Colombian, Cuban and Argentinian. I did not care because I felt more of a learning there than in English. Nevertheless I did see that those professors disliked Mexicans at USC but I did not care, I was learning to the best of my interest. And yes, in Los Angeles, the Mexican capital of the United States, there was no Mexican much less a Mexican American that taught Spanish. There were three Whites—figure that one out—and the one sympathetic White woman Beth Miller was also always correcting me in my Spanish because I did not speak a Mexico City UNAM lingo. I spoke rancho Mexican. Uuuu que la chingada I thought. The others just ignored me. There also was una Uruguaya who taught she was Spanish, a Chilena who taught she was Isabel Allende, a joto Spaniard, a suburban American dream Colombiana and even a mafioso Italiano, but no Mexican much less a Chicano. Maybe Cheech is right, Mexican Americans enroll in Spanish and earn a B. In my case C's, because I learned Spanish through English so my brain pattern was different. The verbs and the nouns switched.

Near graduation was my closes hope and I did read Gabriel Garcia Marquez in Colombian, five or six of his books. I learned he wrote about Colombian history and whorehouses, whorehouses and Colombian history with some references to some French writers and puterias again. That is the tragedy of Los Angeles, there are no overt puterias so our literary imagination is dead. Who wants to write about their maids in Malibu?

Later my friend Guillermo Esqueda would complain why high school graduates had to take English classes at the college level if the assumption is that one has already completed those courses in high school. He would emotionally yell out to my class, when I attended college in Guadalajara in the early 1970's, I did not have to take Spanish courses to attend my one year of medical school. I was already literate.

Don Memo got me thinking, even into adulthood, the empire wants to make sure that English is force fed. The English departments at all colleges are some of the largest; they force students to take those introductory courses; English majors are encouraged to enroll. English departments are the epitome of Whiteness. If you want to become White, major in English. Out in the streets of Los Angeles, the Nahuatl past abounds in the art form of restaurants, street names, city places, communities, in the form of geography from desert to plantas to coyotes to California. Yet in those English courses there is the illusion that White people are back in England not in the Mexican ranchos de California. How practical is Shakespeare in Northern Mexico? Shakespeare gets pushed on us even now more than the Bible. At least in the biblia one can see Mexican names such as Jesus or Maria, Jose or Magdalena, Juan o Elizabeth.

Shakespeareanism gags Mexican Spanish and maybe its good that most Mexicans do not major in English. Those Mexican American English major graduates are the most White washed of any Chicanos I know. Look at Richard Rodriguez, he believed those British books a little too much. Chicanos who major in English or teach English are the most coconuts. These Brown gringos are disgusting to come across. How can a Mexican American have a White identity after the US stole half of their culture? Maybe I am too Apachis, chingado I want to root out the catholico in every Mexican, I want them to worship Jeronimo not Jesucristo; conduct peyote ceremonies and have limpias and ignore all the pinche padre nuestros. The English though irritates me more.

At East Los Angeles College, in the heart of Aztlan, Northern Mexico still not conquered because the Mexican flag flies freely with no one complaining about being anti-American. You drive on Avenida Cesar Chavez and red, white and green abound. Drive on Folsom Street and the flag flies confidently. It is like the last stronghold, el este de Los Angeles has not been told that the Americans arrived. The only other threat is a Salvadorian flag as if they were making their last stand but still sell tortillas and aguacates to the residences. They simultaneously will not sell pupusas because self righteous Mexicanos will not eat that shit and the Salvadorians know this. Where do the Salvadorians think they are at America USA?

But at East Los Angeles College which is not in East Los Angeles, it is in Monterey Park and not part of the greater community, the English department operates as an American Fort of the 1890's. The college forcefully beats Mexicans into their English classes through mental whips. Mexicans want to transfer, graduate, move on and English is their first reaper. They have to take their placement test and fight for spots as if fighting for cheese rations on the reservation. The bungalows are third world and the instructors are majority white. They have two or three Mexicans just to make sure the Whites are acting fairly. No Chicanas! One Mexican hire means five more Whites hired, they hire White females. The dogma begins.

The only reason this department survives is because the classes are mandatory, few Mexicans would enroll in English if they did not have too. The one Chicano Studies department in California and possibly the US attracts students out of interest but the infighting due to divide and conquer methods through one White woman whom they allowed to subvert the department has the third or fourth highest enrollment. English and math alternate as first and second, but Chicano Studies thrives on racial interest and not curriculum imposition.

The English department treats Mexican Americans as if they were wild Indians. The department consists of American Jews, Australian, Irish, and German immigrants and many east coast Whites who could not be hired anywhere else. Why would a white person want to teach next to East Los Angeles?

Solely for the check which means they were nobody's selection. If they want to teach there because of the brown student population, then they are condescending by acting missionarily. How can other immigrants whose English is a second language or those who speak with a heavy accent (Irish and Australian) teach Mexican Americans-technically already Americans English? If most of the students at East Los Angeles College already speak English.

This beckons Don Memo's criticism: why am I wasting my time taking an English class if everybody has taken English from k-12? The answer lies in the fact that Americanization did not take hold in high school so just to make sure and in the beginning of college, English is buggard at us to make sure Whiteness is instilled in our psyche. Even if the White teachers are not US born and have learned their English as a second language, Whites are still preferred over Mexican Americans. The two Mexican Americans are so intimidated of their White colleagues' retaliation, they stay quiet for survival purposes. This might be the only college job they will ever have, they self gag. The immigrant Whites act like they know better. Becoming White is like a baton. Until they arrived in Los Angeles, they had probably never met a Mexican American and were they surprised to learn they spoke English and Spanish.

In addition, what normal person wants to correct essays all his life? Is this his individual contribution to the continued conquest of Northern Mexico? Is he an aspiring writer because I do not recall any of them publishing a book of significant value? English teachers seem like social workers who do endless paperwork to no avail. They just fill out cycles of wasted paper.

And they believe themselves to be better. When in all honesty, the Chicano student is actually much smarter because they speak two languages. Your average White person does not speak two languages, and the English he speaks in California is Spanglish with his Mexican American accent, whether he likes it or not. They do not speak with their draw-yoaw, or their New Yolk much less with a British tone.

What do they really teach? Their lifestyles. In this I question all English departments in the Apachis homeland. My former student Elsa Ramos who transferred from East Los Angeles to UC Berkeley mentioned that she struggled greatly for two reasons: she did not comprehend the cultural context and White professors graded her harder. I tend to believe many Mexicans do not advance because White professors grade them much harsher and White students much easier. The unofficial official failing rate at East Los Angeles College in the English department is 50%, one instructor Alex Immerblum failed 21 out of 26 Mexican students after berating them because they do not speak English well. One of my students was enrolled in the class, he was one of the 5 who passed. A letter of complaint had been submitted but Jews are protected with their racism towards Mexicans.

Later, Elsa mentioned that she enrolled in Chicano Studies literature courses, also in English with the same amount of work as in any White English class and realized that Whites were asking her for explanation on Mexican cultural themes. This is not new, if the scholastic aptitude test was written by Chicanos with questions on menudo, buche, tripas, carnitas, chorizo y calo such as simon ese or chingada madre, Chicano scores would be 1500 and Whites would be complaining about the culturally biased test. Elsa earned A's not C's, even though she spoke two languages.

If English is based on culture, then English courses are centered around cultural thoughts then White cultural thoughts are being transmitted to Mexicans. We do not live White culture, then how are we to comprehend this lifestyle much less their lingo, psychology or sense of humor if they have one. English therefore by omission is cultural death for Mexicans. Thus by force, English mandates are changing the culture of the land from burrito to wrap or liquado to shake, from guitarra to guitar but one can not sing rancheras in English so the canciòn art form dies. Who sings norteño music in English? As my friend Ruben Lopez states;

"English is not an exact science. Two plus two will always be four, yesterday, today or a thousand years from now. How exact is English? Only White peoples interpretation, plus Americans don't speak with thouth, goeth, or thou cometh."

And British culture is the end result but Americans are not English so can one instill British culture through mind-numbing, dull and tedious English literature? All the English departments have British literature as part of their curriculum in northern Mexico, but what does that have to do with rancho California? Would the British come to the US to study British literature? I hope not. There is no British literature in the deserts of California because there is no geographical connection. When has anyone seen a castle here? Disneyland does not count. Do British authors think highly of American literature? Would they call it English literature, or is it watered down English as Ruben Lopez states? Plus how can Americans be English if they do not even like futbol, juego de pelota, soccer or as the British call their national pastime, football.

California State University, Long Beach has a Dutch national teaching some Shakespeare and other British literature courses? Another second language learner teaching in English. Would a Mexican be hired to teach British literature in England or Holland? Nothing makes sense. No wonder Chicanos hate English, there is no relevancy but they like good writing. The most popular poet in East Los Angeles is Morrissey, a British national followed by Zac de la Rocha a Chicano poet himself. They both make you think and thinking is not in the lexicon of the English department at East Los Angeles College, following orders is.

This emphasis on English writing is dubious, in an article by the *Los Angeles Times*, they pinpointed how many White managers and CEO lacked many skills in writing. They had examples of illiterate White color people with the best pay. So were they passed easily with no accountability? Whiteness is the great access card and here it showed.

In a strange and comical way, it is hilarious to think of English departments in California because these are lands where the real learning is outside and not inside much less in a non Uto-Aztecan language. There is so much mental masturbation imbedded in this field because it has no real value within the geography. Is that not the reason most American publishing houses are located in New York? A PhD in English in California is a fictional story of how people invent their own status quo yet everybody knows it is a farce. A lie becomes a truth, everybody is lying to each other, it must be real. When all these English books have to be imported to California then where is the authenticity? Pinche engles mamon!

Let me invent my own PhD, the Julian Segura Camacho Doctoral Philosophy degree. Pinche vacilon!

I was in the Fruitvale district of Oakland with my sister from Mexicali and niece visiting my carnal Marcos Ramos and his then novia, Maria Cruz. Maria was finishing her B.A. in English at Berkeley and understood the fake rhetoric of English. We had just eaten chingon Oakland style— Rancho de San Antonio (original name) Mexican food when my sister and niece asked Maria in Spanish what was she studying at the university. Maria innocently answered as she rubbed chola style red lipstick on, "English." As she answered and continued rolling the red lipstick, my sister and niece looked at each other and were confused. Then they started laughing at the silly answer. They then asked her why she would study English if she was born in San Francisco, weren't you an American citizen. Don't you already speak English? You look real India Mexicana, but you already speak English. We all laughed because it was strange that a US citizen would be taking English classes if most US born people already speak English. Would a US born person take ESL classes? We continued laughing until Maria clarified literature. A Mexican national would not take Spanish classes at the university in Guadalajara or Monterrey. We laughed the whole day over that issue even as we secretly drank Pacificos walking along the Golden Gate Bridge.

Todo Santos, Baja California Sur:

Talavera Shop:

"Come in señora and see our wonderful art pieces we made ourselves. We are from Puebla and our family has been making these for a long time. The plates never scratch and we painted them."

I had to ask them, where did you learn good English, vivieron al norte?

"No, we learned it by watching television. No schools, no books, just hearing what they say. We even learned their bad words: mother fucker, fock you, son of a bitch."

I left laughing, pinche television did the duty of a teacher. The White teacher in English is about learning your place. Only they have the knowledge, even if it is watered down English.

Chapter Three

Mathematical Formulas as Following Orders

The Mayans invented the concept of the zero; the sea shell represented the zero

Guia Turistica, Oficina de Turismo
Chichen Itza, Yucatan

If there was a second subject I abhorred and continue to detest it is the emphasis on mathematic courses. Do not get me wrong, we should know arithmetic, division, percentages, shapes, angles, measurements and how to use a calculator, a device which simplified the world for the world.

In the news, we hear on a regular basis that students continue to fail in math, and Mexicans in particular have been categorized as doing the worst. These generations of low test scores are listed on the State of California website by district and school. The scores indicate the level of barrios from impoverished fifth world places such as Lennox (or unincorporated county Torrance) to Santa Ana or Lynwood to mid-level barrios. By observing the names of the districts, a person from Los Angeles comprehends a racial construct of the place. Compton means Black and Mexican; the Coliseum area Black and Salvadorian; Crenshaw Black only; Santa Monica ethnic white; Manhattan Beach American white; Bell Gardens Mexican American; Downey aspiring whites—fake blond Mexican women. Maybe it is good that most Mexican Americans do not read the *Los Angeles Times*. Why read the social obituary racial caste system they are born into? Who wants to read the obvious?

And those school districts now code for property values and intelligence because somehow those schools will be made more intellectual by the surrounding property, despite that many in White areas are nothing more than White trash consumers. They live by those scores; real estate agents use them as their hook for a homebuyer because everybody wants the best for their children as long as they are not Mexican children. They want to keep their children as far away as possible from these Mexican children because they fear they will bring the intelligence of their children down. The Mexican child will score low and bring down the average score for the school as a whole. They do not want to be stigmatized as a Mexican school.

And it all begins with math and English scores, the tracking system of White Americans to justify who is smart and who is not.

I remember learning math slowly, very slowly. One and two are concepts that take time to learn. I began with my hands and toes, sets of ones accumulated to twenty, but then I had to learn beyond the twenty to thirty and forty and fifty. I learned that the ones would continuously be repeated in each set; the same up to one thousand. Soon I learned subtraction, multiplication, division and percentages. Multiplication I enjoyed because I was good at memorizing, and once I learned the answers, I always knew them. My memorization ability is very extensive but not my algebra process. They are two different thought processes; as the process grew, so did the commands. The teachers made us emphasize the steps, the steps were more important than the answers, but I did not think much of it. By this time, every aspect of school was about "obey" and "command."

We were told when to start the day, how to walk in, where to sit, when to go to the restroom, when to eat, when to play, when to return, when to speak and what assignments to do. The steps were on the board and follow them. We could not really rebel because we did not know what that was especially because that White teacher became as previously mentioned, a surrogate mother. Even if she ignored us, we wanted her approval because we thought in mother-child terms. We would not misbehave with our mothers. When she assigned the homework, I believed that her requests were more important than anything else. She wanted it one way and that was the way I was going to turn it in.

I was taught to be linear, to think linearly with no other perspective. I did not even know there where multiple choices to problem solving issues until I clashed with my mother one day. My mother had always been helpful, making sure I completed my homework. She had helped me out with times tables before, but when I struggled with square roots, she noticed I was frustrated. She walked over and stared at my doings. My mother and I did not clash with your wrong but more of "dejame ver que tienes." She would then state, I used to help your tio Miguel to do his homework when he attended Central High School: "Yo le hacia su tarea," proudly she stated. It did not help she thought he was an idiot who could not focus on a little schooling.

When she looked at my square roots, she stated, "Ohhhh, raizes cuadradas. Mira asi se hacen." As she showed me the steps, I was confused because the steps taken were the reverse. She followed other steps that did not resemble ones the teacher gave, and I was worried they would be marked wrong because the teacher had stated that the correct answer was not enough, she had to see the steps. Even then I thought to my innocent self, what does it matter, as long as the answer is correct. She wanted to see that I had followed her steps, but I struggled with them. To this day, I do not grasp the logic of square roots. Never in my adult life have I had to utilize this skill unlike arithmetic, percentages and measurements. What are square roots used for or algebra for that matter? Will algebra get me a job writing?

Pero mi jefa was all proud because she showed me her steps that turned out to be correct, but I rejected my own mother's teachings. She sensed that I was hesitant and kept stating, "asi se hacen raizes cuadradas." She kept reassuring me by stating, this is how I learned them in school in Mexicali, but I kept rejecting her knowledge as my mother because I was terrified that the teacher would mark me wrong. I could never tolerate failure, I might have been a C/B student, but I never failed a course.

Even then I realized the inconsistency of having a problem marked incorrect when the answer was correct. Yet I was too afraid to challenge, I had to accept that my mother's methods were incorrect while this foreign woman was correct. This is the part that confused me the most. If my mother can help me, then why are her methods incorrect?

Afterwards I was very hesitant to ask my mother for help again because I felt that her approach would be rejected and I did not want to be graded down. Yet it did not feel correct. It did not help that my math skills were not the greatest, so I was working with an inferiority complex too over this issue. In elementary and high school, if you are a math whiz you are considered intelligent; if mediocre, no applause went out for being average. When you are an average student with no superior skills, you are just a body with no individuality or recognition. I was such a body, so I was not applauded for my evening struggles of hard work. Nothing stood out in any subject and in that way I was like my mother, an average person who had not been permitted to amount to anything even though she knew her mathematical concepts albeit in another form that lead to the same correct answer.

As I struggled in math, I slowly closed my mind to this subject because I did not feel it was either practical or useful. I resented the subject throughout high school so much so that I earned a D in algebra II but accepted that is still passing and settled for that grade.

Interestingly, addition and subtraction have been the most useful, and I did not really need to go to school for that, that could be learned at home. Was there an assumption that the home was entirely ignorant, that I would not learn anything there? In a strange way, I was sent to school more to be socialized with other kids versus really learning about that one career that would not arrive until twenty years later. How idiotic is that? My household was not stupid; however, poverty reinforced the perception that we were stupid. Of course, there were other forces in play.

Early on, I understood that the label of intelligence was anointed if you were excellent student in mathematics. (The laudation of students who excelled in math did more damage to me because I did not excel in math and therefore felt inadequate). I learned then there, I was not intelligent and sensed I was dumb because I was not recognized. I was not directly told I was inferior, but the idea of the chosen ones meant that the notion of duality was in place. For there to exist the chosen ones, there had to exist the unchosen ones, the positive and negative, the day and light, the male and female all told me that I belonged to the pendejo group and that did not feel rewarding. My mother did not make me feel that way.

At home, my mother taught me I could dream wildly and the dream was valid. I almost sensed that I was doomed futuristically because I was not as bright as those chosen ones. I wanted to be treated the same as anybody else, especially because I felt that the decision to be recognized was based on the perception of the brain, and I internalized that the characteristic of smartness was rooted in biology and not instruction. I realized that biology could not be changed, and in such view, those students chosen would be preferred for life. I felt I had no hope because I was not reinforced to know that a person can better himself. I would always be average and never selected.

And I never was. Good attendance and service certificates were all I earned, because I seldom missed class and was always accommodating to the teachers as had my mother taught. Yo era caballero desde chico, I was chivalristic from upbringing. Yet that was not perceived as intelligence; it was a second category of not quite good enough and intelligent.

Later in high school, I felt the same dilemma. In my ninth grade year, an A earned admitted you to the honors math courses the following academic year. The teacher was worried more about quantity and not quality. She instructed clownishly with enthusiasm and her hands in the air but cared more about speed learning than learning period. I needed practice and patience, but she depended on your innate knowledge as a sole criteria. I already knew from my 8th grade math teachers; that patience and practice were the key to my success. And I had succeeded even after I moved to the second junior high school.

Yet in my high school experience, there was no patience for learning. Speed learning was the sole emphasis, but much like music, a person can learn the cords right, away since it is practice that makes the cords sound beautifully. So years after elementary school, the process of selecting the chosen ones happened again. The chosen ones included other Mexicans who were culeros because they were naturally smart. Some of them would not even when to talk to me, but they loved their Asian friends, if that was something to be proud of.

I did not earn the honors category, but the school reinforced the honors courses by the simple selection of the honors classrooms and those students remained insular, incestual throughout most of high school. They were also enrolled in the same English and science honors courses. They were considered geeks as a rebuttal from the non-chosen ones. If we are ignored, then our vengeance was to criticize. They were placed on a platform because of adding numbers; I spoke two languages and that mattered little.

This time, being a chose one had more meaning. They were virtually chosen to attend college. They were the prized-possessions of the high school. They were given the special treatment by the counselors and teachers. Their high scores on the Scholastic Aptitude Tests only reinforced their mental superiority. I looked at my score and thought I must be stupid. Although I continued working hard in my favorite subject, social science, there were no honors courses in social science. The fact that I only had one Mexican American teacher in biology demonstrated that we Mexicans were not thought to be as smart as White or Asian people. This one teacher was considered a token because he was that one Mexican who defied all the odds. I liked him because he was tough like my mother was but also soft hearted, Goy Casillas. He was my football coach who was known to be a general, but I know he treated me special. He was not as anal with me. I wanted to do better in my biology class because I did not want to let him down. In his class, I earned a B. Race matters and he showed it to me. Even when I had to leave practice for work my senior year, he defended me from the White head football coach. I would have been punished by Larry Reed, but Casillas provided understanding.

I eventually removed myself from those worthless algebra courses. I earned a D because I did not understand the material; I did not want to waste my time either, for I saw no relevance, no practicality in my junior year. The teacher spoke to the board and the subject did not stimulate me. How was this going to improve the probability of me getting nalga? Vulgar yes, but at the same time, I needed to comprehend the applicability of this subject in life. How would algebra advance me in life?

What I learned in high school was to distinguish between practical and impractical. I was already working at a local supermarket at age sixteen and knew the finances from my father's social security pension. I knew that the money would diminish as soon as I turned eighteen. I knew my mother's budget. How we survived is beyond my comprehension, maybe Usen, the Apache mother deity has always taken care of us without us knowing.

By the end of my senior year, away from the horrors of math (algebra, trigonometry, and others being job securities for White teachers), no math related science courses and an enjoyable history course, I made the honor roll based on my grade point average. Even my Japanese American former Chemistry teacher was surprised I had made the honor roll, as if somehow I was eternally stupid. I accepted my certificate proudly as I neared the exit of my Americanization internment. When I could choose my courses, I excelled; when I was mandated, I was considered not smart.

The tragedy of math courses is that they have no relevancy to life beyond basic addition, subtraction, percentages, measurements, and figuring out your mortgage payment. How is it that we did not learn about the practices of credit scores and obtaining a mortgage in high school or even in college?

My brother Mario Alberto once asked my friend Marcos who works at UC Berkeley: "What does college really teach? They should teach how important your credit score is, how to get credit, how to improve your credit, how to clean your credit score, how not to get in debt, how not to use a credit card, how to avoid bankruptcy or rebuild from bankruptcy because without an understanding of your credit score, you are not going to get ahead in this world. What does the university really teach?"

We all laughed at his street blunt question, yet I thought, the math we take in the US school system teaches us only to follow orders. I learned very early on that the orders I was to take were from my teachers, not my mother. My teachers sought to indoctrinate me in the system—their logic, their methods only. My mother's ideas were wrong and would only keep me behind.

Chapter Four

Traditional Academic Fields Means Whiteness

Any conscious Mexican must always have hatred towards White Americans and the subsequent generations of White people. For many reasons from past to present, from English only to Border policy, for their cultural impositions, for their hatred of our Apache blood, for them still being in Northern Mexico.

Zac de la Rocha, singer and songwriter of Rage Against The Machine, writes that "anger is a gift" and we Mexicans have not been allowed to use this gift nor have we exercised it. We have been historically and are currently despised by our sole presence, both directly and indirectly: from hunger to exclusion to self-fighting to inter-Mexican fighting. We are kept hungry struggling to survive or fighting amongst ourselves, when instead we should be fighting Whites and fighting for the land they took. We find ourselves lost and helpless, and while some succeed, most do not. The survivor mechanism forces most of us to focus on simply eating and providing shelter because even that is a constant threat. Since we strive to survive, we simultaneously submit— submit to our low positions and stay inside our neighborhoods.

Of course, submission begins in elementary school. As I argued earlier, White teachers, English, and following orders based on math are all mechanisms to halt any outside native, Mexican influence from growing. The fact that most schools are still dominated by Whites either male or females demonstrates the manipulative racial paradigm: White people are in control even if they are immigrants from England or Russia. The curriculum amounts to White propaganda of we did something with these lands. The environmental destruction of White people never factors in, but consciousness is not an end product of the American grading system in California.

Moreover, this mental demagoguery perpetuates itself even harder into the higher levels of education. As high school teaches no practical life skills beyond driver's education or typing, we look to the university or college settings as institutions of higher learning; however, these institutions are worse than high school. We have been lied to again.

At this level, the same pattern follows: White teachers now called doctors (because of a PhD.) imbue the notion that they are smarter. Ninety percent of faculty is White, both men and women even at barrio colleges. The administration is predominantly White with one token Chicana.

They rarely make room for Chicanos (proud Mexicans) in the administration mainly because they fear Mexican Americans. And here they make you believe you are also intelligent but never as smart as them. While nobody forces anybody to attend college is their philosophy, the same White racial notion of manifest destiny exists.

Since the voices are Whites either in teaching, and administrating, the curriculum translates into the same reality. Because Whites believe that California is now White land even though they have no historical roots to adobe, the curriculum has evolved into this same White realm of manifest destiny. Jesus blessed them!

When I majored in Political Science, I realized that it was not just political science per say which is an oxymoron in itself. How can bribing be a science? We learned about White institutions, White leaders, White actions, and White history as part of White political science. White presidencies and even White views on foreign affairs. My interest was Mexico, and a White view of Mexico is what I learned. I kept saying to myself that is not the Mexico I know. But they enforced this superficial knowledge.

In my other major of Spanish, half of the department was also White. So I sat and listened to White people with gringo accents teach me about Spanish. And true to their form, they all but ignored Mexicans and focused on Spain or Castellian. That was the first time I can honestly say, I saw White people even with their American accent be somewhat fluent. It was strange talking to White people in Spanish; I was in culture shock.

Throughout my undergraduate education, the White curriculum abounded in all subjects I enrolled in, whether anthropology or even physical education. I cannot say I ever heard the word Mexican American or Chicano in any of my college courses because even the course I took with James Diego Vigil, was listed as Peoples and Cultures of Mexico and only to be a mild version of Chicano Studies via USC style, in Reagan form. Vigil was my only Chicano professor in four years of undergraduate school in two different colleges, and he watched his every word.

Graduate school at UCLA was no different in Urban Planning. Fake former hippie professionals and pseudo intellectuals who professed to be open-minded and progressive but on White issues only, referred to Brasil only in Latin America Studies. These professors would show their Whiteness when challenged for their lack of people of color material. I was advising them on some books that I had read on my own, but they did not see that recognizing Chicanos as natives was important. Even Mike Davis in his book *Magical Urbanism* criticized the UCLA Planning School for the omission of Chicano Studies curriculum that had a long history of racial studies and urban observations of Los Angeles. The college instead jumped on the Gloria Anzaldua and Cherrie Moraga bandwagon almost ten years after their publications came out but failed when not comprehending that the lower Rio Grande Valley in Tejas and lesbian issues are not the only factors Chicanos faced, much less in Los Angeles, California.

As I exited graduate school, I realized that these White people have no connection to real life beyond their secluded White suburbs. Yet most importantly; I saw their bigotry was very obvious.

The real shock for me came when I applied to the Political Science Departments in community colleges and realized that they only hired White folks. Previously, I taught Chicano Studies but beyond two classes; (one dubious under anthropology); I was not really a Chicano Studies major though I did piece meal a Mexican focus but always on my own, not from any faculty mentors. I had read vital Chicano history books because I could not get that anywhere else. Besides at UCLA, there were no graduate programs in Chicano Studies, only Latin American Studies that sort of mentioned Mexico but it was still deficient. The Mexico emphasis of Latin American Studies focused on the Salma Hayeks or the Jorge Castañedas but not on everyday Mexicanos from Los Angeles. They did not know what to do about Chicanos and Juan Gomez Quiñones in history had been an awful example of Chicanos at UCLA. Thus, I had to make my own Master's program and I did.

Therefore, I used the knowledge I gained from reading and endless preparation plus my own family history. To show examples through my farm working family was a way of connection, along with being raised as a Mexican American albeit not from East Los Angeles but el Rancho del Centinela on Ballona Street in Inglewood.

Eventually, I got hired to teach Political Science, and I soon realized they wanted a White voice. I could not lie in the classroom, and racial exclusion was not something they wanted to hear in Political Science. How could I speak positively of a political system if most Mexicans and Blacks had been excluded through poll taxes and literacy test?

Just as I renounced teaching that subject, Chicano Studies part-time positions became available and at times courses through the history department on Chicanos courses. I would never be given a course on US history unless it was an 8 am course as occurred at California State University, Long Beach or a last minute change at CSU Dominguez Hills. I would not be hired again in those subjects unless in Chicano Studies until I realized, these sons of a bitches have segregated me into Chicano Studies only because that is where Mexicans are allowed to teach.

Even when I was given a chance to teach Cultural Geography or Cultural Geography of California, the White fake liberal chair of Bill Selby of Santa Monica College was regulating me like his boy. When I did not abide by his White titles and definitions, he switched my class. When I argued that Mexican culture was the foundation of California culture, after three semesters they were writing me up. He referred to Mexican culture as Hispanic, ignored the Apache Mexican entirely. How can a White person judge culture when he has no culture? The Doors, tequila and tacos? We got into a fight, and for one class it was not worth it. What amazed me the most was how they went out of their way to write me up because the White curriculum of lies is so well-embedded that they fear the truth. Of course, the whole Earth Science department was made up of Whites only. Even my friend who works as a provost stated, the administration was powerless to regulate their hiring because they had full union protection. To me, unions are like country clubs under the guise of protecting working people, White people only.

Soon enough, I realized that unless it stated Mexican American in the title, I was not going to instruct in mainstream American universities. At first, I felt inferior about only teaching Chicano Studies, but as I became conscious I realized, I was going to teach chingon in Chicano Studies and use it as a platform to critique Whiteness.

And I did. I invented the academic term of "White Nigger" to deconstruct White people's racial power structure of Mexicans. I had earlier come to the realization from my Chicano Studies courses on colonial Mexico that the way to deconstruct negative terms and themes is to apply them directly to the oppressor. In this case, Catholic Spaniards, I still refer to Christianity as superstitious, paganism, heathenism, northern African Arabs in defense of Mexican brujeria. We Mexicans practice witchcraft, so what, at least we do not believe somehow prayer will save and that somebody is really listening. In my world, that is insanity.

The same applies to Americans: cultureless killers, racists pigs, mojados, wetbacks, joto/faggot culture and White niggers as they called Mexicans niggers too.

If White professors can use the words "Illegal Aliens" in the classroom, then why should I not be able to? Mexicans have been so whipped into their place, that they are afraid to defend themselves vocally. And we turn the other cheek. Bullshit, does not work for me because that is not America. If we are not fighting, throwing chingazos, then we will get plastered by evil White people. Unfortunately, these are the laws of the land, I did not invent them. I try to comprehend them, but I must also survive. In war zones, peace activists have no place.

I have concluded that when departments refer to art, biology, education, sociology, music or psychology, these are all euphemisms for White art, White biology, White education, White sociology, White music, and White psychology. Just as Chicano Studies refers to Mexicans and even that they are trying to Anglicize by lumping the subject with all other Latinos, as has occurred in the department of Spanish.

And White these departments act in the same way as when the US arrived to the northern Mexican child of California. In the CSU Long Beach Art Department, there are no Chicanos while there are over 50 full-time faculty positions. This is not unconscious racism but an overt fuck you and your murals from East Los Angeles attitude while they study endless hours of Rembrandt and Picasso. As if they were Americans.

White people assume themselves to be the norm socially, so their academics reflect their White nigger selves. And because they presume to be in total control, they ignore the fact that there are still Mexicans who know their history and are present to counter their "boy" attitude. I am not one of those writers that provide them the benefit of the doubt, White people consciously act with malice and hatred towards Mexicans, but because they have the power and have partitioned the goods, it is very difficult to challenge their supremacy.

Just as Whites have controlled from elementary on, they continue to do so in the university settings from handing out PhDs to hiring White faculty to the White administrators. White women are not innocent bystanders, they use their bodies to entice and bribe and have no sympathy for us Mexican men and women. They think they can talk down to us too. A White woman will never raise her voice at me, I will put her in her place solely through fear.

Why are White people still the majority of college graduates and Mexicans the least likely to graduate from college? People are favored by race and civilization and awarded through easier grading and passing. Why do White people have the majority of PhDs? Their White professors sign them off with no hesitation. Why are the majority of faculty White? Because their White counterparts hired them.

The same in reverse exists for Mexicans. We are their servants, and they want to maintain that racial social order at all costs. There are even Chicanos who have high Scholastic Aptitude Tests scores and have been denied entrance into UCLA or UC Berkeley. They keep a lid on how many Mexicans are admitted. At CSULB, the administration caps the number of Chicanos admitted and are quick to tract them into remedial courses. How can Mexican Americans who are bilingual be considered inferior to White trash students who only speak one language and attend college as if it was an extension of high school with dorms? These White students attend college to experiment with narcotics, and engage in gang group sex, and run wild in the dorms.

White faculty, White minds, White books, White departments amount to White learning. The call for multi-ethnic education is an indication of the narrow focus in White higher education, but the minimum is all they will do. They have jumped on the bandwagon by including homosexuals as part of the multi-ethnic curriculum, which should never have been allowed to occur. White people want another advantage to being White for their lifestyle and cry they are persecuted? Where is the logic?

How is the White joto/faggot community denied their citizenship? And why should he be granted a special privilege because of a sexual act? Since when does a sexual act grant anybody special privileges? Heterosexual men when horny are persecuted by the law for looking for a woman, and I do not see us seeking a special amendment. Cars get impounded, they get arrested, and they are socially branded as sexual deviants.

Whenever I meet students who are majoring in traditional departments, I always challenge them by asking them how much have they learned about Mexicans. I use their answers to encourage them to enroll in Chicano Studies courses because there, Mexicans are the center of the classroom if taught correctly and proudly and not White. Interestingly enough they state, "Yeah, we have been trying to find relevancy in the courses, but we want out because we are so close to graduation."

The lack of relevancy is very visible in other fields such as Philosophy: Greek thinkers but no mention of ancient Mexicans such as Ce Acatl Topiltzin-Quetzalcoatl or Jeronimo among Mexican Apaches. Architecture does not go beyond the Egyptian Pyramids even though the base of the Temple of the Sun is wider in Teotihuacan, along with ruins such as Toltec Mayan Itza people: Templo of Kukulkan or Uxmal. Ancient Mexican architecture was astronomical too, but the Greek or Roman ruins receive more lecture time defined as Humanities or the Classics. The Apache Ramada along with adobe structures are more practical for the desert than wooded homes and fancy cardboard boxes known as drywall. The ramada protects a person or the house from the direct sun, but White general contractors build the trellises only to suffer from the scorching sun rays that penetrate the crevices in the summer time. Likewise, during the rains, one cannot sit under the open trellis because the whole patio is getting wet. It is beautiful to sit under the ramada and watch the rain come down. My grandfather built a ramada with an enclosed sloped roof that protects us from the sun and the rain. Where are his architectural contributions?

Europeans do not use a porch or sun protector over their door, I saw this in Holland. The door opens up with nothing above it. People generally remain in doors not in between under a beautiful ramada.

The ancient Mexicans had invented a solar and lunar calendar more precise than the calendar with the Jesus Christ birthday imposition and his twelve gang members. The Aztecs and Mayans had twenty day calendars that accounted for the leap year based on day signs. The Jesus Christ calendar emphasis uses his disciples mixed in with some Greek deities and has no consistency. One month there are 30 days, the next 31, the other 28 but every four years 29. If you were born on February 29th as almost happened to my cousin in 1972, you age only once every four years? And superstition abounds, there should be 13 months but there is fear that the Christian White world would have to recognize Jesu Cristos' wife or the number 13 is a day of evil. White cultural impositions even if based on north eastern African myths.

The same occurs in music. The world of Classical music comes from Europe; this I know because in elementary years we always listened to symphonic music of Mozart and Tchaikovski but never to the rancheras from my house. And we are stigmatized. Even as Mexican Americans, the notion of bringing ranchera, banda or norteña music to a university classroom is comical and embarrassing. Once in my Spanish class on Mexican music, I had to pair up with a Tejano who always told me he was part Spaniard. We did a group project, and he turned out to be ashamed as I played my Banda Sinaloence music. His face turned red, the whole class got uncomfortable at USC, and he even complained that I had imposed my will on the music selected. And I did. This is the native music of the desert people of California-Sonora-Sinaloa. Banda from the 1970's was not sung nor did it include string instruments, puro air and tambores. We danced and hymned the music. I was proud because I did not back down. I was raised with this tradition.

Mariachis is more Michoacan-Jalisco-Colima and Guanajuato music. We were norteños and we loved our Apache music. You should have seen my mami Luz danced to those tamborazos, una chulada.

And once as an instructor, my former students who were part of a banda called, Banda Sol de Santa Cruz, performed for my class at Long Beach State. This was the first time a banda Sinaloence had performed there. Nobody knew what to think of this experience, but I loved it. Two weeks prior, they had performed at the Sundance Festival.

If a Chicano wants to learn norteño music, would he go to UCLA or Long Beach State? Could those White professors teach Mexicans how to play mariachis or conjunto? A local cantina could provide more Mexican cultural comprehension than those White professors; they cannot even speak Mexican Spanish in Los Angeles. My three Chihuahuas and my Pekinese: Tixoc, Luna, Xochitl and Simon Ese understand both Spanish and English, what is a White person's excuse? Just in case for on the record, the guitarra and violin are Mexican instruments that were exported to other parts of the world. They both originate in the lush Mexican forests of Michoacan-Jalisco region in the mountains along with the Huasteca region for the violin. Children learned to play while they worked in the countryside. The wood and the intestinal animal strings came from geography. If you doubt me, the word Mariachis means music in Coco—the Jalisco people who originated this art form and the word Chis means land and is found all over the interior of Sonora and California. Plus when has anybody seen Mariachis from Spain. Los Angeles has more Mariachis groups than all of Europe combined. The growth of guitars is amazing: the guitarron, the vihuela, the requinto, la acustica, el tololoche and the arpa.

On a recent trip to Mexico City, I bought a small arpa the size of a checker game board. I asked the man where had he bought it and he told the following: I invented it. I am a music teacher behind Teotihuacan and in the school I put it together along with the songs I have included. This hortizontal arpa is an amazing piece. What do White people have, the banjo which is really a North African instrument?

It is no coincidence, college graduate Chicanos tend to resemble more Whites in likes and taste and have the same anti-Mexican anima as White people. Yet those Mexicans like my mother and father and grandparents who did not attend college are more Mexican than even those Mexicans in Mexico City. My mother has not lost her Mexican accent in English y que. She sings Mexican songs beautifully, she makes the best tortillas, raised five sons as a widow, practices her Apache brujeria and somehow and someway has never lost her love for the land of California as a Mexican land. She taught me to eat chile and nopales y frijoles con gusto and that no university could ever teach me. My mother bestowed upon me the PhD White people never could—a PhD of culture and a love for the land with all its good and bad. I have retained my Mexican culture and am learning how to play the guitar from other Mexican Americans who have learned it from other Mexicans solely for the preservation of ancient Mexican songs.

White people always question Chicano Studies by criticizing our Mexican focus as if their White paradigm was superior. What Whites and their puppets (Asians and Blacks) do not see is how their exclusionary curriculum and hiring practices have forced us to fight back. Whites will continue to be White. And higher education is a place for Whites to maintain Whiteness.

What value does higher education have for a Chicano?

Chapter Five

Race Determines Class: Marxism is a White Paradigm

"I have been arguing all my professional life with White faculty that race is more important than class, but they just dismiss my point."

James Diego Vigil
Conversation in Whittier

"M.E.Ch.A. also experienced division in the ranks; members moved in different philosophical directions, pursuing such ideologies as Marxism, socialism and feminism, he says."

Cal State Long Beach group celebrates 40 years of fighting campus discrimination. Phillip Zonkel, Staff Writer, Long Beach Press Telegram,

October 5, 2007

There are in essence two major patterns of analyzing so-called American society. One is the direct conservative Anglo Saxon Protestant mind of individual property ownership. Whiteness is part of the American characteristic which is why Europeans, at least the Anglo Saxon derivatives keep receiving open entry while an Eastern European Turk is limited by admission.

This is based on the castle identity of Great Britain that even until today distinguishes between Welsh, Scots and Irish. To my eyes, I do not comprehend the difference at least based on neither appearance nor culture. They all seem to have the same features and traditions within an island or next island over, the same accents and the same living style. I comprehend religious differences but sometimes I cannot comprehend the difference between a Catholic Church and an Anglican Church except for the occasional Anglican female priests.

The birth of the American tribe originates with this psychological background but is distracted by geography. North Sea Europeans can be tribal in their castle as it is their historical home but in a Nahuatl continent, the same rational cannot exist. They were in somebody else's land and people lived there and yet they killed them. As they killed them (Creek, Cherokee and Seminole nations) the new Americans established a legal narrative of who could be citizen. The notion of citizenship was defined in 1790 as White People, based on the continental name of the western hemisphere. We Mexicans are going to move to France and because we do not like in between yellow and dark olive look, we will not include you and because you live in the continent of Europe attached to Africa and Asia, we will then name ourselves Europeans. We are the new nation called Europeans. Ridiculous and yet it occurred.

The White people prerequisite was rooted in the English castle definition of Eng- Sa(x)ssen from Sassenheim in south Holland and not Catholic. Protestant means not taking orders from Rome anymore (from Mediterranean Africans), but we'll keep the robes. This has been the criteria of an American but Mexicans know they are Americanos, too that they will never call an American, American, they will say, gringo, gabacho or estadounidense but not Americano. America exists all the way to Tierra del Fuego. English descendent people did not care that they invented their nationality because deep inside they were still Anglo Saxon Protestants. The east coast still believes that way.

However, the more they traveled west, south, southwest, northwest and south they altered their identity. The closer they remained to the east via South or Midwest—Ohio and Indiana, the more Anglo Saxon they remained. The more they traveled into Northern Mexico, the more Texan and Californian they became. White people in el norte identified themselves as Mexicans called themselves in their homeland. This does not mean they stopped acting Anglo and Saxon and Protestant, the Republican Party of California up into the mid 1990's acted in such 18th century manner but Orange County still believes they are the last stronghold of the Saxon dream warding off the invading Indians from Los Angeles.

It is of no coincidence that the most Anglo Saxon Protestant regions of the United States are in the south and the mid west, the bible belt as my brother calls it. Their voting patterns and religious behavior dictate such characteristic. One cannot purchase beer in Oklahoma on Sundays. In California (Northern Mexico), Sunday is when most beer is purchased. Oklahoma is the south west but not that many Mexicans categorizes it more Anglo. Tortillas and carne asada are not the social norm in Oklahoma as is in Tejas. White Texans might hate Tejanos but they dress like Mexicans and like their tamales, unlike gringos in California.

The redneck or the hillbilly is the descendent of the Anglo Saxon. This is what they have created, but as my brother David's father in law Ed stated in Okmulgee:

"I might be a redneck but I ain't no hillbilly, lets get it correct." White people have standards too, get it correct.

The Anglo Saxon Protestant is an ever-present force that still shapes the United States where they have been the majority, and in the classroom that milieu is part of the norm. My criticism of White departments was mentioned in the previous chapter.

The Anglo Saxon Protestant is what Samuel Huntington is attempting to protect under his Harvard realm of Who Are We? But at least he is direct and straight forward. How does he explain Black people being Anglo but then again, the Anglo mother land has its own share of Black Anglos that speak no different than their White counterparts? There is always room to grow.

This is the rule of the land but the counter to such attitude are the other realm not as prevalent as the millions of Anglo faithful in the South and the Midwest but still vital in the study of academia.

For clarity, this is not an analysis of Europe, but solely the foundation for my criticism of Whites who believe class is more important than race. The flip side of the Anglo Saxon mindset is the workings of Marxist who study the US based on societal interpretations by the German Karl Marx, himself a Saxon, but I wonder if he saw himself this way. Deutschland!

Sometime after the death of Karl Marx in the late 1880's, academics began to interpret his analysis as panacea for the social changes and struggles of their time. Part of this was driven by the labor movements that sprung forth as industrialization was taking place in Germany, England, and the United States. But this class struggle was not new and had been rooted from the Roman era via the slave classes that had existed into North Africa. The Africans were not as communal as they make them out to be.

The Karl Marx readers such as *The Communist Manifesto* seemed innovative from that noble perspective of the king owning all the land and the relation between vassals and peasants. Both were really country people depended on cattle. One milked the cows while the other played on his horse and kept guard. Few owned the land and as factory worked ensued and the horrors of repetitive overseeing labor became instantly evident people rebelled. Or as a Mormon missionary mentioned, when a few in society have the majority of riches the others will reach and take it.

In the US, this seemed as a viable solution to comprehending the growth of industrial America along with the union efforts. This was all studied and hence Marx becomes the academic tool to attempt to comprehend the structural forces. Throughout the 20th century, history and sociology departments have employed Marxism for studying all American historical periods. And the social sciences have been quite receptive to this new field.

Part of the Marxist acceptance was to comprehend what the newer bodies of European immigrants who made their way in to the US were doing and surviving. They were attempting to analyze the class differences ever present in American society from the moment, property owners were part of the requirement for American citizenship along with being White.

Still class warfare became the ever-present theme in history reproductions because 20th century European immigrants also did manual factory labor. In the process of their analysis and intentionally omitting, they were admitted to college because they were White; class becomes the only lens by which to comprehend American society.

Everything is class, class division, and labor strikes. However, many other vital factors have been excluded. The first being the denial of race and culture. How can race and culture not be part of the analysis in higher education when laws were set by Whites to eliminate Brown natives?

Returning to the 1790 citizenship clause, White was spelled out. And for those Creek landowners, no matter how much land they owned, they could never be White citizens and not be protected by the new white government. From 1790 to 1978 of my lifetime White Americans have engaged in Imperialism and colonialism, but those terms are too obscure.

Just as Osceola fought to keep Whites out from Florida, and eventually was defeated, my grandmother Kika was also defeated through eminent domain laws in Inglewood. She owned the land in north Inglewood with my two other Ninas Josie and Emily. They were uprooted and sure my Tia's received some cash, but their memory to the land where their parents had lived was lost.

I was raised from age 9 to 15 always hearing my Kika (Francisca) cry how they were lied to by the city of Inglewood: "They told us they were going to build a post office and instead built warehouses." She would always cry and I stared at her helpless. My Ninos-abuelos went from living on a one-acre rancho with three houses on the lot to living in a small one bedroom apartment where they could not raise their chickens, have dogs and more important a little space. My first birthday was celebrated in my lost land. We went from living on our rancho to being crowded into modern slums to be.

This is what White academicians miss. The human consequence of being displaced in your own land while newcomers with a different skin and customs do as they please. The American turmoil of land concentrated in a few hands was solved through the expansion of the White people into the Cherokee, Seminole and Mexican nations. Race was the determining factor. Nahuatl people were killed and Whites moved in through an orderly land lottery. That is how Georgia was given to White people from land taken from the Cherokees. This was not a class, but a continental racial issue. The displacement of people was be-cause of their race as was the enslavement of other people because of their race. This is not a class issue. White people were not being sold on the auctioning block or being killed for standing on the land where they had been born.

Where White people relocated and starved to death? They caused the starv-ing and the death.

The same rational applies to Northern Mexico. Mexican people had lived on these lands for thousands of years, had farmed and developed some of the most extensive agriculture in the world. Had knowledge of water irrigation, cuisine, architecture, of the climate, had founded most of the modern cities of today in the so-called west, but when the US Army invaded, the real war be-gan after the war ended.

White Americans stole the land that these people had been living on for thousands of years. In this case, Whites were whether rich or poor were given Mexican lands that benefited Whites only at the expense of Mexicans. This was not a class issue rather an invasion by European people that benefited them, while Mexicans were reduced to White slave labor if they were fortu-nate to survive the racial genocidal war unleashed by the American invasion. How does Marxism specify White poor people fighting to overthrow the orig-inal Apache Mexican owner? How does Marxism explain genocide of Mexi-cans in California, Chiricahua or Mescalero Apaches?

In the period of American dominance, how does Marxism explain the use of Mexican labor to benefit Whites through cattle or agriculture on lands that use to belong to them? Marxism cannot explain these contradictions because it was never meant to be for Mexicans. Mexicans were already more or less communal people who bartered more than rely on paper money. This was true of Apachis or Zunis or Navajoas or Mayos. Even the ranchero class of Cali-fornia had more of a communal system where cows were allowed to graze collectively, you word mattered as a legal document and geography served as a marker of spatial divisions.

Class was not as defined unless in the areas that were more Catholic but that was centro Mexico, and even then, those people still ate tortillas as they do today. Value based on racial pigmentation was not a measuring tool for in-clusion. Racism arrived to Northern Mexico when Americans arrived. How is that explained? As the cultures clashed why was it acceptable for Americans to outlaw Mexican traditions. Even today, there is no bullfighting ring, no peyote ceremonies, Spanish is abhorred, rooster fighting criminalized and street vendors persecuted by the police for attempting to survive. Only Ralph's or Albertson's can sell oranges.

From the end of the civil war, Whites have been given access to land, and Mexicans, while we have received hatred in return. The following industries:

mining, cotton, cattle, construction, railroads, orchards and later factory work have all depended on low wage Mexican labor. Unions historically excluded Mexicans and have never truly represented them unless to make money off of them. Even today, the most powerful unions protect White people: teachers, police officers, faculty, nurses, Hollywood, governmental offices, while employment that Mexicans are casted into receive no protection.

Even when a union member, they will sell you out as happened to me when I worked as a cashier or a faculty member. The union took sides with the employer. The faculty union refused to represent me and was not legally obligated to do so when I was rejected for tenure at East Los Angeles College. Four years of mandatory dues were more of extortion. Ultimately that is what unions are, private sector money makers protected by the government to protect the White middle class.

How does Marxism explain the role of racial segregation imposed by Whites over Mexicans and Blacks? In Texas, the bathrooms in courthouses stated, "Baños Aqui" for only Mexicans to use and my grandfather Gus stated in the mid 1940's he would see signs that stated, "No Blacks, No Mexicans and No Dogs Served." He once told me that they on one occasion entered a restaurant that did not serve Mexicans and left when the waitress told him they would not serve them; this was Los Angeles. There were pools that permitted Anglos only, no Mexicans. In Arizona, my good friend Abel Amaya mentioned about his upbringing in Douglas that any haircut would have to be across in Agua Prieta because in Douglas, Mexicans could not get haircuts due to segregation. Fortunately, the Mexican barbers had better style, but the rejection was there.

Abel also encountered segregated restaurants. He protested the restaurant by intentionally sitting down, opening the salt and pepper shakers, and when the police arrived, he and other friends turned the condiments upside down, spilling it all over.

Abel even attended a Mexican school where the quality was inferior. The conditions of the White school told the real picture.

How does Marxism explain the 10% cap on success of Mexicans earning $50,000 or more while immigrant Dutch or English succeed within their lifetime as recent arrivals to the US? Or the simple fact, that 90% of professors are White in the University of California, California State University or Community College system, White women included.

These White professors professed to combat class and an end to class divisions, but are the first to mandate that one have a PhD to be considered full time in their little country club. Tragically, even the few Chicanos that have a PhD like Luis Arroyo at California State Long Beach believes that all the full timers should meet this criteria without looking widely at other qualifications.

Full time lecturers are not advocated for in Chicano Studies while in the history department where Whites make up a majority, they are. Whites take care of each other no matter the class, while closing the door on Chicanos unless she is a woman for self-convenient purposes. And yet those PhD Chicanos hold other Mexicans to tougher standards while simultaneously advocating class unity.

There I have two angers, first, the hypocrisy of the degree and the institutions. I do not have a PhD but I have written three books on Chicano issues and am not valued both by my kind and obviously Whites. But the other danger I see stemming from Marxist thinking is the brainwashing in telescoping the world only through class and places of work only while ignoring race and barrio. I have been analyzing race for Mexicans for twelve years because even college graduate Chicanos continue to struggle for employment, live in barrios and digress economically. I too have gone backwards. In 2000, I earned $73,000 but today-tax year of 2006 I earned $53,000. How does a $20,000 drop occur within a period of five years when I have the most years accumulated in instruction, I have four books published and this one on the way?

For me racial exclusion is my answer. And the fact I do not see White barrios in California while variations of Mexican barrios exist from impoverished to in between to better off indicates a racial stratum for Mexicans. Whereas Whites have reached somewhat of a parity, there are no White barrios; Mexicans live in trailer parks. Whites are still the highest earners in the state and half of them are immigrants to the US. Whereas Luis Arroyo, the PhD in history as he mentioned to me stresses class divisions but always behind, race factors in. Wake up and look around Cal State Long Beach, that is the racial answer, but he is still not convinced because he is too dogmatic that class is the divide.

Those Marxist professors make you think White and Luis is an example of doing research on furniture workers which he as been doing for five years but cannot think for himself at a time Chicano independent thinkers are needed. In those five years, I have written seven manuscripts and have published three books in fifteen months. What is the difference? I was thought to think for myself by my mother and not White professors. I might not have the secured employment but my ideas are now at Harvard, Yale, Stanford, The Bancroft Library at UC Berkeley, the Library of Congress, Columbia, UCLA and many Cal States.

And not to solely pick on Luis Arroyo, others fall into this category. Mike Davis is a good example but for other reasons. Racially speaking he is more ahead than Luis, but because White people on their own talk racially while in public they act racially silently. Their acts reveal their racism. They hid under the unconscious umbrella but the silence is their protection. White academi-

cians have come out on racial history but they want an easy class analysis solution. Mike Davis falls into this category. When he writes about the Anglo
Saxon Protestant power structure that has not died, he seeks simple categories
of workers and now Latinos. He should know better than anybody else that
Mexicans and Salvadorians or Puerto Ricans are not the same. Especially because he knows that Mexicans have been in Los Angeles for eternities that are
desert people and Salvadorians are recent arrival immigrants from the trop-
ics. Two countries over from Mexico. They do not even share borders to
claim a common cultural heritage. Yet he links them without acknowledging
we are racially and culturally different.

Part of his ignorance is that he does not speak Spanish and he has not paid
attention either. We do not like each other. Chicanos are a national minority
and Salvadorians recent the attention and have begun their Americanization
process as other groups have too. And just because a southern Mexican needs
a job and the US interfered in El Salvador does not mean we are the same.
The US has never ceased terrorizing Mexico on both sides of the border. Second, what did the Salvadorian lose to the US?

He creates great errors by artificially lumping us together. What if the Mexican is dismissed from his job and he has to look in another type of employment, does he now get merged with the Honduran or Guatemalan. I know
Mexicans from Chiapas who do not see themselves related to Guatemala but
somehow we are to say yes they are. How arrogant on our parts? He further
ignores other scenarios, my mother and I do not see ourselves related to peo
ple from Zacatecas or Oaxaca, too different in culture and customs. We are
more Apache-Californians and they would say the same thing about us. I frequently get asked more what American Indian am I than Mexican. I tell them
Mexican, I am both. The Treaty of Guadalupe Hidalgo applied both to the
Zuni and the Catholic Mexican from San Jose. All desert people are Mexicans
not Americans.

He once lumped my first manuscript that he quoted in his book Magical
Urbanism as a second generation immigrant? How am I a second generation
immigrant? That is an oxymoron. My mother, father and I were born ten
miles apart in the Imperial Valley divided by an armed fence and my grandmother is a Sonora born Mayo Apache. How can I be an immigrant in the
same desert where my grandmother was born and where my great grandmother is buried? We cannot migrate from California to California.

His Whiteness and sure his work got him his faculty position at UC Irvine
but we will see if I am given the same opportunity by Whites. Will I be hired
full time without a PhD even though I have published four books and two
more are on the way? He does not have a PhD, but he's applauded even though
he left out Chicanos in his *City of Quartz* book (a book about Los Angeles).

He focused more on the Black and White paradigm. He is applauded for having been a truck driver. Does sitting on your rear constitute work? I drive all over as a freeway flyer in addition to having done some bracero work. I picked cotton as a teenager, I started working at 16, I worked the graveyard at a supermarket, I did my eight month stint as gardener at age 14 with a circular push lawnmower, I helped raise my brothers, I use to wake up at 4 am to take my mother to work, I have been unemployed and lived off my one ex-girlfriend by borrowing money, I never received any scholarship for college other than loans and paid my first two years at El Camino College; I was not even suppose to transfer and I was the labor help as I paid to help put a new roof on at my home.

I paid and worked because I never had quite enough income to fix the 1938 duplex that had not been remodeled since 1938.

Marxist professors ultimately are the Philip side to the Anglo Saxon Protestant because their academic results assist in the suffocation of a racial analysis for Mexicans and blame our caste position on class. I would argue that race determines our American class and not the other way around because we Mexicans once owned the land in a non market manner, were much more equal, and roamed freely with no mental blocks or faux categories of intelligence. I do not believe ancient Apachis needed a PhD to eat, the land was all there for them even if they had to farm, hunt and fight. No White people permeated in our psyche, our nightmare had not arrived; I still cannot awaken from this pesadilla-evil dream.

Chapter Six

Cholos Sin Barrios: Non-Mexican Latinos Obliterate Chicano Studies

Los Mexicanos de Los Angeles son ojetes, no son amigables.
Mexicans from Los Angeles are unpleasant, they are not friendly.

Waitress, Sanborns Restaurant, La Casa Azulejo, Mexico D.F.

Claro, cada uno cuida lo suyo.
Sure, each one protects their own.

My Mother's Response
Monica Segura Camacho,

The discussion above took place the on the first morning of my visit to La ciudad de Mexico. My wife loves el D.F., she states you still feel the Aztec vibes on the cemented lake bed of Texcoco; walk into the cathedral and you can tell the Catholic Church is built over an Aztec structure. You can feel the slope as you walk in the church. Nobody wants to admit to her observation, it could destroy modern Mexican colonial Catholicism by reviving Mexica cultural thought. Christian Mexicans might have to confront their identity crisis.

I am ambivalent about Mexico City. Not because it is not aesthetic, I think it's one of the most beautiful cities in North America. For me, it is too much a city. I feel out of place culturally because I have a rancho view of Mexico and el D.F. does not fit my description. I have a Baja California/Imperial Valley coyote Cucapah, Chicano below sea level view of Mexico. To be in an urban metropolis high in the mountains is a culture shock to me. So are the traditions. I am too much a norteño Apache.

Fortunately, this feel is not without reason or logic. For the first time in her life, my mother was able to visit Mexico D.F. None of us knew what to expect in her reaction, including her. From the north, she hears much negativity from the media and southern Mexicans who migrate north, thus as any normal Mexican American, she was apprehensive in her excitement. Always over looking her back, in a state of Chicano paranoia, I am the same way, I constantly fear the unknown because we were raised in Los Angeles and the Imperial Valley. White people act like the overseers they are, and Chicanos follow act out such animosity. The defensive look until they feel safe. Mexican American mistrust!

Interesting enough, my mother loved Mexico City. The negative reputation was a hoax and just American media defamation of Mexico. We knew better, we lived in a neighborhood where drive bys and extreme Mexican poverty made all of us ashamed, what was there to proud of by living in the US. Lennox was one of these barrios that God forgot about or was too busy saving others except us Mexicans. Even my friend Ruben from East Los Angeles on Folsom Street was shocked at the extreme pobreza, but he loves the burritos de carne asada at Tacos Acosta on Imperial Highway.

That first morning, we walked over to the old house of the Viceroy during the Spanish era converted to a restaurant. My mother walked around with a Mexican film gaze rolling in her eyes in amazement once inside. In essence, this search was a life long dream for my mother to visit Mexico City. Mexico City was as exotic and unknown for us as New York City, none of my mother's family was from that area and even though her grandparents were from Guanajuato, they were dead by 1947, the year of her birth, that my mother strictly views her Mexican existence through the lands of California. It is all Baja California.

We sat down and were served; my social skills in place and conversation took hold. The waitress asked us were we where from, Los Angeles. And then a little conversation and the observation from the waitress. The waitress mentioned that other Chilangos had mentioned to her that Mexicans from Los Angeles were not friendly and with her pardon, we were assholes. I could not deny it but simultaneously; most Mexican nationals have been aided by Mexican Americans either through work, cultural adaptation, neighborhood welcoming even if unceremoniously. Its not as if Whites would welcome Mexican nationals into their barrios because they did not invite us Mexican Americans either. How many Chicanos ever visit Manhattan or Hermosa Beach?

My Nino Gus would always state that had it not been for Mexican Americans many Mexican nationals would not have received any assistance or even their US residency that only hinders Mexicans.

When I mentioned to my mother what the waitress stated, her response was in a calm demeanor, "Claro, cada uno cuida lo suyo" (Sure, each one protects its own). My mother continued enjoying her pilgrimage and my wife and I just laughed at my mother's Apache wisdom. I instantly comprehended the logic. You mistrust any unknown intruders. The Cholo philosophy of life, protect your space, for your space is your identity. My brother Mario's famous words for lost Chicanos were to call them "Cholos sin barrios." You cannot be a cholo with no barrio. That spatial designation is who you are, your space identifies you specifically and all of Mexico functions the same way. Why would Los Angeles Mexicans be different?

Many people from Zacatecas, Michoacan or Jalisco wear their pueblo designation on their vehicles. The Zacatecas decal informs the world they are from that land and therefore they are that space. Mexicans view their space religiously and Mexican Americans view their religious space even holier because they have to live with an occupier that denigrates them with no respect for the land other than to cement it and commercialize it only to ravage it later for another venture project.

My mother as I learned from the trip was visiting an important space for the Mexican psyche yet always knew what land she was rooted from. The most fascinating aspect apart from ordering tacos de pollo and receiving taquitos de pollo, we realized "our" Mexican food was nowhere to be found. It was difficult to find chiles rellenos. My autistic Huntington Beach guero brother-in-law abhorred at the difficulty finding chiles rellenos. At the rooftop restaurant of the Hotel Majestic with its beautiful aerial view of the Zocalo, John bluntly stated, "What kind of Mexican restaurant is this that they do not have chile relleno." His Mexican American grandmother Emma Holguin from Clifton, Arizona always made him chile rellenos. In his suburban white world of Huntington Beach he can always find chiles rellenos.

That is the first lesson for any Mexican American visiting the final destination for the Anazazi Traveling People who came to be known as Mexica: Mexican food is the food of southern Mexico. No tortillas de harina, no frijoles pintos, black beans only and no carne asada or machaca. Carne asada, machaca, tortillas de harina, frijoles pintos, chiles rellenos battered in eggs with no salsa on top is straight, papas fritas, pollo frito are all Chicano Apache foods of food of Northern Mexico. Those Chicanos whose parents are from the center of Mexico know this because they live this dilemma. They do not have burritos de carne asada in Jalisco or maybe they do on the ranchos as Don Cheto states.

As we visited el Zocalo, Teotihuacan, Xochimilco and I saw my mother interact with Chilangos, I realized and they informed us that we were norteños based on our appearance. My mother was asked by a brujo in the Zocalo if she was from Aztlan. The geography does give you identity. If one ever looks at those maps of Native American cultures through the US, along the divide of Mexico from Mexico, the word Apache runs from el Pacifico-Tihuana including Los Angeles, across to Yuma-Mexicali, Nogales-Nogales-El Paso-Juarez- San Antonio-Laredo-Reynosa to Brownsville and Matamoros. Apache is the type of Mexican culture prevalent in these lands. Not Mayan, not Chilango, not Tapatio, not Zacatecano, not Cora or Purepecha, much less not White (is this a culture), Black, Asian, Centro American, Caribbean or South American.

Nobody comprehends this dynamic except for southern Mexicans who move north and the term is "move north." My grandfather/godfather Gustavo did not consider any of us Michoacanos, he considered us Sonorenses, Apachis del norte. I always sensed that was why he came north, to reunite. The Apache faced genocide, and the heirs have had to confront in the 20th century the American hatred of norteños. The land feeds you and because you eat the minerals of the land, the land provides you with the appearance of her.

Southern Mexicans who move north, even if their children are born in Mexicali consider them Cachanillas versus Tapatio. I met a family from Guadalajara in Tonala who referred to one of the daughters as Yaki. I asked the older sister why she called her by that name and she stated to me, "ella nacio en Cd. Obregon, Sonora es Yaki. Esa es su tierra natal." I was stunned but it makes sense, you are that land. Cachanilla people from Mexicali where the Yuma and Cucapah Mexicans abound take this name from the native plant. My sister always points out the Cachanilla plant every time she sees it with pride. For she is that plant, Tihuana and Ensenada residents have also taken us this identity because the plant is native to Baja California.

I love the Imperial Valley, both El Centro and Mexicali because this is my land, the land I was born into. I cannot be separated from this space. I love Los Angeles though I hate the rape by Americans of this land because mi Los Angeles is part of the land I was born on. All I have to do is follow the Cucapah mountains south and head east in there in that ranchito I was born. I love mi Baja California, I cannot be separated from this land, the nopales grow natural, the coyotes roam freely when not cemented over and the aguila flies in the air. The baseball team from Mexicali are known as the Aguilas and their stadium is called the Nido, the nest. My nest is California.

All the ancient images of an Apache Cucapah reflect a bandana with long hair. I put one on with my long hear just to stare into my past. We are told we are not this or that when ultimately we are Mexican Apaches. The Mexican flag reflects our desert past, the eagle in us and the earth in us. We see ourselves symbolically there because this tells us who we are. Americans want to kill our desert existence either by our denial or amalgamation with other brown people who have no ties to Aztlan.

My Nino Gus was a fair skin Michocano but the sun does not burn you there the way it does in Sonora but to my amazement, when we sorted through his belongings, we found two paintings of Apaches or Indian warriors as most would call them. At that moment I understood his connection to the Apache Nahuatl world whom remained ever defiant of not allowing Americans to assimilate him. Even in his coffin he wore his sombrero to the grave. It was beautiful to view him die in Aztlan and be buried with his Mexican rancho Chicano Michoacano pride. He could have returned to live out his final years to Zamora, but he considered his homeland Los Angeles, and in Aztlan this lost child was buried. My mother stated the image of the Apache I have hung in honor of my Nino Gus is alive, she could feel the energy of the Indio radiating off. She felt the same energy radiating forth from the image of a picture of Jeronimo in an article about the decapitation of his head. I felt the same power. I felt his sad eyes staring at me that I had to place it down. It was too painful to see. Americans have a fascination with Mexican heads: the heads of Joaquin Murrieta, Pancho Villa and Jeronimo have all gone missing. My bruja mother stated, there are some spirits that can never be killed even in death. "The spirit of Cuauhtemoc alive and untamed," as Zac de la Rocha says.

In Mexico City, they could identify us instantly because of our height. My mother and wife are both 5'11, my brother-in-law is 6'0 and I am 6'5 and weigh 325 lbs. They could spot the tribe a mile away.

And in that beautiful pilgrimage to Mexico City, we were always reinforced we wore norteños, Aztlan, el homelands of the people that settled in what is now an urban metropolis. So north I return always knowing this is my motherly land eventhough outsiders want to tell us different including non-Mexican Latinos.

Because of my Apache bloodline, I cannot accept an imposition and a false amalgamation with strangers based on the artificiality of Spanish Catholicism. My names are not Spanish, they are Mayo

The Chicano experience must therefore be understood within a geographical racial culture experience based on blood and birth not on immigration. Most Mexican Americans are Pacific Northwest desert Mexicans. This is evident in the statistical fact that most Mexican Americans are US born. More than 65% are US citizens therefore to deny this existence is academically incompetent or diabolically misleading. If we were in Tejas those Mexicans would be Chihuahua-Coahuila or Gulfo people of Tamaulipas. I focus on the deserts of Sonora because this is my location.

Hence the Mexican American experience is based on being desert people but also conquered people with race and culture continuously under siege manifested through barrio conditions but also a rancho barrio identity. The barrio community identities reflect the survival strategies and spatial limitations of being Chicano-Mexican American in California. El Centro, San Ysidro, Logan Heights, Escondido, Santa Ana, Wilmington, Inglewood-Lennox, East Los Angeles, Highland Park, Coachella, Casablanca, Pacoima, Jim Town Whittier, Southgate, La Puente, Bakersfield, Fresno, Ventura, Oxnard, barrio Santa Barbara, Santa Maria, Salinas, Seaside, Hollister, Soledad,

Coalinga, San Jose, San Mateo, the Mission District, Fruitvale barrio in Oakland, Stockton, Sacramento, Modesto, Manteca, Antioch and even Santa Rosa all reveal a spatial, racial, cultural and indigenous connection.

Why are there 15 million Mexican Americans in California? Did we just arrive? Why is the typical meal tacos fritos, papas fritas y una torta de jamon (hamburger) the most typical common food? The hamburger clause is wrong, why is there no ham in a hamburger rather beef. Una torta de jamon. In Holland, which is closer than Germany to the US along the North Sea, they do not eat beef patties with bread or cheese. In Delft, the waiter looked at me strange when I asked him for bread and cheese. Merging cheese to your bread with cold cuts is viewed as odd for the Nederlanders, but not for us Mexicans, we put cheese on everything. Queso is queso for us, the quesadilla. My Mayo Cucapah grandmother would add queso to the top of the taquitos. When Mexicans state yellow cheese does not go with their tacos fritos, they are not desert Mexicans. The Chicano Apache Mexican American is his own cultural creature that even southern Mexicans do not comprehend unless they marry into them or are raised in Sonora or Baja California.

This historical racial past therefore must be comprehended based on the experience of being Mexican American. This is what the Chicano Movements were about, for there were many. But as colleges paid lip service to Chicano issues, and the creation of Chicano Studies took hold for the right reasons, which was to study the Mexican American Chicano experience. Not the Latino, Centro American or Puerto Rican experience. An anti Mexican resurgence has taken hold since the mid 1970's.

Certain evil animas cease to die as long as Americans continue to live in the Apache homelands. And one way to counter demographic growth of Mexicans from California is to allow other people in through US Immigration Laws. The arrival of people from Latin America (Mexico is too Nahuatl to be Latino) created an easy escape clause from a national minority to an immigrant group much like Salvadorians or Hondurans. The US had no more moral obligation to US born Mexicans.

Therefore, since the late 1980's, the world of Chicano Studies has gone from urban and rural Mexican struggles for survival in California to the immigrant Mexican. This has been perpetuated primarily by White academicians who have been keeping track of how many Mexicans move north while they have ignored the infiltration of European immigrants. Los Angeles has the third largest amount of Canadian immigrants. That means a large number of Whites are not Americans by birth. A Naturalization paper is not citizenship, anybody can print out certificates on their printer. How is this a country based on culture?

But Mexicans are counted as if we were a ticking time bomb. Blacks do it too. I remember former Speaker Willie Brown state in the late 1980's: "the names Jose and Maria are going to be the typical California name, not John and Mary." It is almost like the "one the little two little three little four Mexicans, five little six, little seven Mexicans" and the number has gone into the millions that White people are alarmed of too many Mexicans, but we are suppose to be dead. I liken it to the one Black friend clause by Whites, but Chicanos do not really want to socialize with Whites. I don't, I find no connection.

And as White academicians have limited the number of Mexican Americans into their program, those chosen are done so with the purpose that they can parrot White ideals into Mexican thoughts, I mean, Latino. Four decades after the Chicano movements, Mexican American departments have lost their Mexican identity. In conversation with Roberto Cabello, editor of Floricanto Press, he has mentioned to me why he is interested in my writings. He stated to me, "Nobody writes about Chicano Mexican American identity, its gone dead. There needs to be more works written by Mexican Americans." And Roberto is a Chileno so if he can view the crisis from a publishing standpoint then we should be worried.

But no, those PhD Chicanos have bought the Hispanic Latino imposition led by both the federal government but also daily presses such as the *Los Angeles Times* (beautiful Spanglish) to ignorize the reader into killing the Mexican American/Chicano identity and succumb to their impose term of Latino. "Latino immigrants" is the new catchy phrase and some Chicano academics have been allowed to participate in the mockery of Mexican Americans.

All the new PhD hired in the last five years to teach Chicano Studies whether at CSU Long Beach or CSU Los Angeles are using only the term Latino and are afraid to mention the word Mexican or Mexican American. They at times will use the word Chicano but mock me for using the word Mexican American, as if to imply I were some conservative browny. But they use the word Latino which is in essence the ultimate betrayal of the cry for inclusion based on a Mexican Nahuatl identity not a European or American imposed name.

And to become more historically relevant, the word Chicano and Mexicoamericano referred only to those Mexicans born north of the border. It was a simple cut and dry view but it made sense because even if born in Mexicali or Tijuana, some socialization there, protected you from the contamination of White America. It also meant you were culturally altered through the Pocho term. Chicanos did not refer to anybody else and much less Centro Americans.

They had their own identity, they had not even arrived. Until this day, Centro Americans should not be included in the Chicano debate because they do not have the Mexican American historical connection. Are they desert people?

The Carlos Mencia or the America Ferrer (Real Women Have Curves) people bother me for this same reason. Hondureños by birth or by mother. Carlos Mencia argues that his mother is Mexican but if he was born in Honduras, he's not and he was not born on this side nor in Mexico so where is his Mexican. Second, he states his father is Hondureño and German. For us Mexicans, to be Mexican you have to have both parents. The sperm and the egg must be Mexican. This existence of being mixed never existed for us California Mexicans, if it did you were not Chicano. You can not be Mexican if your mother is White, does she know how to make tortillas or speak Nahuatl Spanish with the Chicano accent in English, eh in front of every sentence.

This insults and denigrates my existence. It is killing me and watering down my concept of duality. No, those mix Mexicans are not the same as me, because both my mother and father were Mexicans. I was not raised with mix cultures or rivaling traditions. I would not be Apache if I did not have both parents. That is my essence even if the rest want to critique me for preserving my uniqueness. Do not take the "he's just another Mexican" approach with me, because I have something valuable, even if only I comprehend it?

In addition, Mencia himself stated that when he moved to East Los Angeles at age 12, he could not identify with other Mexicans because they made fun of him and he's the one who had a green card. Do Mexicans really need a Costco like card to prove they are desert people? He does not know the Chicano experience because Chicanos do not come from Honduras?

Second, his usage of the term "beaner" or "wetback" is downright ignorant or idiotic. Pinche estupido pendejo. No self righteous Chicano that I know because I am one and no one in my circle of friends ever uses these terms. We do not accept the American elimination of the term Mexican, much less accept insulting historical terms used against us. White people know these are fighting words, which is why they only vocalize them in private. I will fight if ever called these terms. Pinche pendejo idiota hijo de su chingada madre, Carlos Mencia uses the words because he was never stigmatized by them, why because he's not from California and he's not Mexican. White Americans still do not know where Honduras is at unless they were in the army?

Why are there no derogatory terms for Centro Americans? Because they have no history here. And even then, they are being socialized to belittle Mexicans which is why they hate being called Mexican. I do not want to be identified with them either.

America Ferrer who portrayed a Mexican American female in the movie Real Women Have Curves continues to prove the social hatred of Mexicans by Americans and the new plastic card members via Hollywood. She stated in an interview to Ilan Stavans, another token Jewish Mexico born American (they don't exist) that she was raised in the Jewish (which means White) west San Fernando Valley and she could not relate and did not have the East Los Angeles Chicano experience unless there is a movie role that will promote her career off of a Mexican character. The Benecio Del Toro Tijuana police officer role was insulting and heinous in the movie Traffic. His lines in Spanish made no sense, Puerto Ricans alike are not Chicanos even if you live next door to Santa Ana. That does not qualify.

In the case of Ferrer, the movie director could not have found a Mexican American actress to portray themselves. I see them all the time in my classrooms. Second, the movie was flawed because East LA Chicanos do not travel 20 miles across Los Angeles to attend Beverly Hills High School, I should know, the Normans were our rivals at Hawthorne High School. Eastside Mexicans try to get into Schurr or Montebello or a Magnet High School, San Marino would have more logic, but Chicanos have a hard time at Alhambra much less in the soon to die heart of the Anglo Saxon world, now called Asia.

So two non-Mexicans benefit from historical Chicanos struggles. Would that brujo in the Zocalo refer to a Centro American as coming from Aztlan the way he did with my mother?

Here is the tragedy of the current state of Chicano Studies. They did not have a barrio Cholo Apache mentality that protects their spatial dimensions. The lure of Latin America arrived even though they had never traveled there, and with a diminished Mexican American identity of themselves, they were quick to forget the fade of the term Chicano and accept Latino with no hesitation. "Hispania is maybe right next door to caucasia," George Lope explains to those confused.

It was easy to say Chicano when others were also doing it. But as soon as the Cardboard Revolution ended as my friend Oscar Barajas stated in his book, everybody forgot who they were for the new X-Box. The real challenge to being Chicano is not 1970, but today 2007 as the very meaning of the Aztlan Mexican is eradicated only to want to be accepted in this Post-Modern world of fake globalization. So when the Chinese arrive, those ashamed Mexicans will be Chinese, then the Martians, Martians, then the Brazilians, Brazilians, then later the Dicks, Dicks. When does one take a stand for their barrio, even if it is only mental?

In 2000, I was at a fun raiser for the Chicano Studies department at Long Beach State University, when then chair Luis Arroyo addressed the political contributors and gave a speech that argued it was time to add the word Latino right next to Chicano. I was hesitant and something told me I was right and the Chumash Papago Mexicana next to me felt the same vibe. She did not say anything but that was the wording.

Luis gave the speech as if he was somehow making a new declaration of the Communist Manifesto, in the process this lost Mexican of the 1960's was justifying the invitation of foreigners without knowing who they really were. Do normal people invite strangers into their home? Do you open your wallet to give away the money? And yet Luis did. He hired a Puerto Rican who has brought in a Bolivian who teaches Chicano identity, like he knows; a Costa Rican woman; self righteous White woman who married a Guatemalan; and now another Centro American male to teach some course on Centro Americans from the University of Wisconsin in Madison. To be fair, other Chicanos were hired but with a Latino mentality and identity who agree in the denial of our Mexican Apache past.

Lastly, to be politically correct, a gay Native American specialist who calls himself a Mexican Indian but wants to spend more time in Native American studies, where all the professors except for two women are White and the students are gringos. Are Mexicans and all people from south of the border to the southern tip of Argentina one and the same?

Luis opened up a hornets nest with no vision or foresight. I have been fighting the Puerto Rican who became chair as he has endlessly tried to deny my rehiring by bringing in other Mexican females to directly compete with the courses I was teaching. And we have fought because they do not like my pro Chicano heterosexual male stance and now I am also fighting with the two righteous Chicana women. Fortunately, the Chicanos all dislike the one full-timer so much and dislike of her is not without merit. Plus, a former professor who left the department stated the full-time English literature specialist was huevona, lazy.

If Chicano Studies is premised on the notion of Mexicans and their experience, then why are non Mexicans being allowed to teach in this field? Are Whites allowed to teach in Black Studies. Mexicans are not like anybody else in Latin America. We are the only desert people.

When I fought with the Puerto Rican in the department, he argued that he hired a Chicana because she was earning her PhD in history who was studying the farm workers. Forget about the fact, I had 13 years of Chicano Studies teaching experience or even the fact that I came from Chicano Californians who themselves were farm workers and participated in work stoppages during work actions led by Cesar Chavez. She should have been asking me questions. But I would not matter as a primary source even though my birth certificate from Imperial County states father's occupation, Tomato Packer. The books written by Whites and White influence Chicano writers would have more merit than me who was born in El Centro because my birth coincided with the lettuce harvest. But I have not been anointed by Whiteness with the royalty title of Dr. Maybe the newspapers are more credible even-though they interviewed people like my grandmother or father. But that does not mean anything. What a tragedy. I never knew Puerto Ricans were from the deserts of California or Sonora. I thought Boricua was in the edge of the middle Atlantic Ocean, forgive my ignorance. Is there a historical Puerto Rican neighborhood in California? Does Irvine count?

Luis Arroyo with his PhD in history from UCLA committed major errors that are not redeemable because of union protection of faculty. They are protected but he is too embarrassed to protect Chicano Studies the way a Cholo would protect his barrio. The Cholo is more rooted in his Mexicanness than this PhD in Chicano Studies.

When I mentioned to my mother that in 2001 Chicano Studies hired this Puerto Rican, she stated, "Que pendejos, ahora el va a traer a su gente." She instantly replied, how brainless, he is going to bring his own people in and before I could tell her he had brought his own people in, Monica's wisdom had come forth.

Just like she stated in Mexico City, people protect their own, I wish these embarrassed Chicanos had the same philosophy and protection for their own because as my brother says, they are just Cholos sin barrio. They have no connection to the land and by accepting the word Latino, they are directly contributing to the killing of the identity and word Mexican. Our own people are killing our future and the academic leaders are contributing to this violent overthrow of the mind. When organized crime groups such as the Eme pushed the Italians out of the east side, they protected their spatial enterprise, but Chicano Studies at CSULB acts with no urgency or sense of protection. What is Mexican has no value. But if Mexicans are pushed in Spanish or even a Centro American course, would there be instant rejection? We Mexican Americans cannot defend ourselves.

Our numbers are already low in the teaching field of academia and here we have a department for ourselves. But we have been forced by guilt to open it up to strangers. What do we stand for? As of right now, the loss of what little was obtained.

Chapter Seven

Chicana Preferential Treatment

"A Mexican woman has the ability to hide because if she marries a white man, she moves out of the community, and better yet if she marries a rich white man, she moves up and out of the community to a suburb where she can be the "Hispanic" on the block."

Mrs. Camacho

"Women pick the men"

California State University,
Long Beach Chicano Studies Major Student

"Aveces ni las esposas saben lo que los hombres sufren en el trabajo."
"Sometimes, not even the wives know how the men suffer."

Monica Segura Camacho

"Women marry up; you won't see a woman looking for a husband in the GR (General Relief) line."

Reuben Lopez

In 1964, after the many Civil Rights marches of Blacks in the South and the "We are the world" protests between Blacks and Whites in the northeast part of the US, other pressures began to escalate from the Mexicans in these lands from California to Nuevo Mexico to Tejas. Lyndon Johnson was quite aware being from Tejas himself, he was conscious of the existence of Mexican Americans.

Lyndon Johnson was also aware of the doubt that existed in his presidency after the assassination of his former boss, John F. Kennedy. Lyndon had to win over many sectors of American society and he did so by the Civil Rights Act and Voting Rights Act of 1964. In the meantime, the old forces of the Anglo Saxon conservative sector did not want to be left out. As Lyndon called in his bribery skills, what we Mexicans call the mordida, he proved that he was a master of it because White men invented bribery they call politics. And Lyndon Johnson defined American bribery. In this time period, through archived bribery, President Johnson made this indolent body do something they rarely do, work. I can just imagine Johnson under the old White male network, "Remember I did this for you. Remember those women. Remember how I helped you? Remember, I funneled money into your account through extra curricular efforts, remember? I need this from you." And those White males from the South and Midwest, livid as they were obligated to abide because White people in power, know the badges of power.

In the American political sector, only Whites can bribe because it is a racial club. Is this not what Blacks and Mexicans in their cultural landscape demanded? Equality is a euphemism for "let me have the same opportunity whether legal or not." As one former PRI employee from the city of Guadalajara stated to my grandfather and I, life in Mexico became worse under Vicente Fox, because only his stalwarts can engage in the mordida. According to him, under the PRI, everybody had a chance at the mordida, not just PAN people. We laughed at this waiter's comment, but sometimes the raw reality is so truthful all we can do is reir.

Angrily Whites voted, but as all White people want to protect their racial superiority ultimately, (which means through laws that favor their wealth or expand it), they voted for Lyndon's acts but without having their say in the legislation. Angry Southern senators voted but to maintain racial supremacy, white women were added in the racial category. White women were now historical disenfranchised people like Mexicans and Blacks.

Those White senators knew that those White women would be protected under Affirmative Action laws and that would also advance the great wealth inequality created through racial preference. Whites and even immigrant whites were advanced, and in California, those immigrant whites now considered themselves the new landowners of Northern Mexico. Somehow White women by the stroke of a White male were now equated to be akin to Mexican Americans.

Did White women work in the fields with a bandana around their face and awake at 3AM to catch the field bus? Did White women pick cotton? Did White women wrap lettuce? Did White women pick grapes? Did White women work as maids for minimum wage in Pacific Palisades? Were White women segregated from swimming pools that stated no Mexicans? Where White women denied service as occurred to my grandfather in Los Angeles in the mid 1940's? Did White women work in sweatshops that my Nina Kika or my ama Monica worked in? Did White women live in the barrio of Lennox? Did White women work in construction or in a foundry as my father? Were White women harassed by the US Border Patrol? Were White women made fun of because of too many children? Were White women insulted because they spoke Spanish? Were they drafted to Vietnam the way my uncle was and had the whole family terrified if he would return? Their gender saved them.

If the answer was no to any question, then why were they included as Affirmative Action candidates? As is stated in the Congressional Record, it was to halt any progress Blacks or Mexicans could make. When the law came to be enforced, the decisions were made based on what was perceived to be needed. In the Black communities, public agencies opened their door to those Blacks and they arrived. The City and County of Los Angeles proves the point here. But in the Eastside, the argument of not including Mexicans could not be stated, they too had been included. At least within the confines of the greater barrio. Where Whites were majority, the affirmative action card was extended to White women.

Even today, every time a White woman becomes a CEO or appointed as the head of a public agency, the word is spread like the bible that progress has been made. A White woman went from Vice President to President but that does not mean she was excluded. Hillary Clinton's presidential bid is hailed as some great progress, she is already in the Senate, and a person cannot get more privileged than her position. She is now simply being driven by ego; had she moved up from being a maid and a speed freak, I could respect her but she did not. Let me be the Vice President of Academic Affairs at California State University, Long Beach. Now that would be progress, but no, the previous person was a White woman who had been in that position for forty years, and in her place, the campus hired another White woman. What progress is that? The institution is still controlled by White people, regardless of gender.

The end result for Mexicans in this façade produced a 90% exclusion from any meaningful alteration as opposed to the 100% historical exclusion of Mexicans from American society. Affirmative action did not end my grandmother's continuing field work or guarantee stable employment for my father or mother. My father spent the mid 1970's to 1980 struggling with off and on employment in Los Angeles. I remember his struggles —working one week and not the next week. More important, I remember my mother leaving the house for employment and leaving us unattended through no fault of hers. Survival was the rule of the law and yet they somehow managed to feed us. My father believed in the intervention of the state, he thought food stamps were a great asset simply because there was food. From a survival perspective, he was right. As long as there is food and shelter, we should be happy or at least tranquilo. As an adult I see his point of view. Why does anybody need luxury when there is hunger? Three pairs of Levi's and endless t-shirts, underwears and calcetines, that is all I want as an adult today, plus some sombreros Mexicanos.

And those were the wonderful days of the height of Affirmative Action in Inglewood, California. The mecca of the Black middle class, but the denial of the existence of Mexican lives even though we had been there before Blacks or Whites arrived. Unemployment, underemployment, roots in the front yard in a dirt quad with no grass and strange neighbors who had no connection to Los Angeles either than plastic card admissions via the airport.

There was no progress for any of us Inglewood Mexicans. For us Inglewood Mexicans our path to absolute poverty would begin with Ronald Reagan.

And yet, I can state, that some affirmative action had taken hold in my father's family back in the Imperial Valley. First and foremost, my father was a second generation Mexicoamericano, who preferred the Mexicano more than any other term. He was a second generation Chicano field worker. He knew the routes and harvest seasons up and down the state. He might have been a potato picker in Oregon because in July of 1969, the clan in Sacramento debated heading to Oregon or to Oakland where other clan members lived, the Hippie Mexicans, his cousins. Oakland won out, but the stress of movement ate at my mother. At the height of Affirmative Action, there was no assistance and there never would be.

Eventually, my mother saved my father from field labor by simply returning to her home region, Inglewood. She was his Affirmative Action and so was her tia Esther. We were not immigrants in the traditional definition. I was third generation on both sides, but survival was primary and Americanization seemed to matter little here.

The Affirmative Action assistance for my father's clan came to two of his sisters and his mother. My grandmother somehow, through work (was field labor enough guilt?) Qualified to purchase a home in the early 1970's (where she still lives) through a government program. The street is called Villa in the city of El Centro in the northeast corner past the railroad tracks. I still know the back roads in between El Centro and Calipatria. That is the only house I have known of hers, besides her little vacation house in Mexicali across the border. Even today at age 81, this thirty-year farm worker veteran travels back and forth between both homes.

The house on Villa Street sits on a large lot where the alleys are still dirt roads, yet this house has four bedrooms and two baths. That house is the rescue of the younger generations, my father's two younger brothers who have just been beat up by Americana and only find security in her. How did she get the home? Affirmative Action. Many new homeowners need some modest assistance. She was not the only one; two or three years later, my father's older sister Rosa had been able to purchase a nice track home where the Castillos still live in. This place was in Calipatria where you opened the sliding glass door in 1977, and you could see miles of beautiful open eastern California desert. But, before the purchase of the home, my tia and her family lived in a one bedroom shack that was falling apart and where the beds were the living room. We lived no different, but we seemed not as crowded because there were only three of us and not four.

Another sister, Maria Luisa we called Licha married and moved one block over from my grandmother's place. Maria Luisa had been one of the fortunate ones because she was able to get a job at the Vons Supermarket while the men labored away in the fields of heat. She was so pendeja and stupid at the same time because she would tell my father not to go through her line for fear the manager might find out they were related. He was a customer, what did it matter? I am modest, but one aspect of Mexicans I cannot stand are those who are arrogant and pretend to be superior. Even today, Luz, her mother calls her sarcastically "la millionaria" because she still owns that property which she rents out and lives in Brawley. Who is she trying to kid? What has made it worse is that she is also a born-again Christian. A fucking Jesus freak while her daughter had a child in high school. Plus, she also believes she is better than everybody because she earned a college degree through San Diego State in Calexico, but the last time I saw her she was still a cashier.

The point here is that three women in my father's clan were given access to property while my father, the second oldest brother was not. He worked just as hard and had done so from age 14. I believe he was saved from the Vietnam War because they could not track him down through a high school. There was no farmworker tracking system, they moved up and down the state laboring for everybody else. My father as normal people do, married and expanded his own family. And his family needed something similar, but when he applied for similar housing he was denied. In Inglewood, there was no assistance either.

This had major consequences because had he been able to purchase a home, there would have been a sanctuary for his children. In 1980, he died and there was no sanctuary. The house would have been paid off through housing insurance, and we would not have spent the next five years moving around five times. Later, when we settled again in a place for 13 years in Lennox, it was evident that we were moving backwards. I could see it based on the neighborhood. We had never lived in such depressed, dense, compressed, third world squalor homes in the heart of the West Coast American city, Los Angeles. I was always depressed because everybody who knew us before realized we were digressing. And my mother who needed Affirmative Action, did not receive it either. And she needed it for her offsprings and piece of mind.

This case brings up another issue: exclusion even within gender. Did White women mean to advocate for Mexican American females? In my mother's case, was it not visible that she needed some kind of assistance to support her kids? She had skills (fashion designer, interior designer, chef but her skills were not valued nor well paid to survive.) During the 1980's, my mother scrapped up food from damaged throw-away recycled unwanted useless food donations, that was our Affirmative Action. Many cans given to us were smashed, label-less, generic, outdated and cereal boxes taped up with warehouse masking. I felt suicidal at times, helpless and angry all at once. In reality, I still am angry at White America (will be until I die) and no compensation today can ever, ever, heal the humiliation I felt and saw my mother go through. As Affirmative Action continued to die and it did the day the primary breadwinner died, I saw the progress Blacks made symbolically in Martin Luther King Holidays and everyday life, but for us US Mexicans, life continued to worsen.

America took my innocence away and never took me in as one of its own. I also knew people saw this place as progress. Many of our neighbors were rushing for their amnesty and their green cards. It was always tragic to hear of Mexicans who could not travel to visit their loved ones. They longed for their Mexico, but my Mexico existed in Los Angeles not south of the border. We were not from centro Mexico. We were third generation Califorences. I always knew we were different because we did not live the immigrant experience, nor the 1986 IRCA plan.

And yet, I knew I was not American either even if on paper I was. Those were dark years for my mother, and I do blame it personally on Reagan and the Republicans. They were the anti Mexican American party, and so were the Democrats. The difference being that the Republicans just voiced their racism. For later Mexicans who arrived from centro Mexico, they had not had the experience we Los Angeles Mexicans did, so we differed. They saw the US as hope, but I lived it as hell. So what if Reagan gave them papers, they were only thinking of themselves not of the collective hurt of US Mexicans. With that mentality, they were just as much a danger to US Mexicans as was any Republican. But thankfully back at Whiteness put them in their place to comprehend what US Mexicans and long term Mexican nationals already knew—Mexican race matters. Some white nigger will always let you know no matter if they profess to be "a liberal" or not. White people are only liberals for themselves.

As I entered adulthood via the workplace, I saw the Affirmative Action question but more out of obligation than sincerity. When I entered the workforce, I noticed immediately there were some expectations of males. I worked graveyards as a cashier with other men. There were no security guards. I could have easily been held up for money, but I guess I was fortunate. In Hawthorne, the extreme poverty was not visible but two blocks over somebody from Lennox could have held me up. Mexicans are not as criminally proned as they are made out to be, but there were people who shoplifted. I refused to play security even though sometimes others did. My logic was, if he is hungry than he should be applauded for running the risk of being arrested. Interestingly, no woman was required to work graveyard, but us men were. No woman loaded the diary box or stocked the store over night. They arrived at 6am and some did light stocking such as medicine. And even though they were promoted equally as men, when heavy labor was expected, the 30-40 lb. dog food was done by men. By me, because I was 6'4! The second store manager was a White woman. It's not as if they were entirely excluded.

My mother would not have had the same experience as one Mexicano señor named Antonio who was the eternal boxboy. The man was a hardworker, was in his late 40's or early 50's and was still a boxboy. I sensed he was too Indio looking for them, but the blonde chick Laura whom I went to high school with was promoted to cashiering over him because he had a heavy accent or over another Mexican American named Henry who was considered too insecure. I hated seeing Henry denied his promotion because I could see his Chicano embarrassment. In Antonio's case, he had this Mexican national confidence that being born in south of la linea gives you. I love that philosophy of "Me Vale Madre." Antonio was not embarrassed by the ugly orange vest or his bagging groceries. He was paid on a different scale, he laughed with everybody and continued with his life.

Yet, Henry was more painful to me because I could see his Mexican American insecurity due to being Chicano. We used to have these discussions of who advances and why, but his three promotions were always short lived. I noticed that he was never given the opportunity to fail, while Laura as long as she fixed herself up with a little makeup and kept dying her hair blond, pretending to be glamorous would be protected.

Henry was half way through El Camino College but stuck in the ever Chicano terror math class. White teachers intentionally fail Mexicans or set up more math prerequisites to justify their superiority and scientifically prove that Mexicans are inferior. It's in the scores they say, but if Henry had cleavage, I don't think he would have had trouble. Clerking was not Einstein-level work, scan and the machine told you the change. Henry combined his hair with gel Chicano style, Einstein never combed his hair. In my upbringing, proper hair grooming was expected even if only to step outside. The White management made Henry insecure, and I saw it as a 17 year old. He was not disrespectful but courteous, hardworking, articulate not a trouble maker, why was he not promoted? I never knew the answer, and those Whites acted tribal as I learned from working graveyard.

I hated them which is why I was transferred to a Black store run by the Irish immigrant nigger store manager Ralph Buehler. Twenty miles away! The fancy Whites and the acceptable female Mexican were transferred to the White Boy's Market in Marina Del Rey; I was sent to Vermont and Slauson, the heart of south central Los Angeles. It was a punishment for defending a Mexican man the Whites were trying to beat up. The man had complained to me of the mistreatment by one of the white trash clerks who later developed cerebral pulsy, Usen castiga. I told the paisano to hit him and leave like a ghost. He hit the White trash culero but was tackled by another Gil Joe White trash asshole. I broke it up and the paisano left, the Whites never forgave me, but I'll be damned to ever let that happen. The paisano violently vented my frustration, so I was going to protect him. And I was punished by being sent to the Blacks.

In this Boy's Market in South Central, I could feel the force of Whiteness and the force of gender at work. I hated that place too and the kiss ass Mexicans and Blacks who thought this was the best they could do. We were not solely judged on merit; we were graded on obedience. I filled the milk box faster than anybody and yet they were not content. Most other Mexicans took the "yes sir" attitude, and some women were promoted to bookkeeping and payroll, which was not difficult because they trained them to do their accounting. And yet these Mexican women considered themselves superior. They were too good to even talk to us, but buttered up to the White manager. I was eventually fired, but I despised that job because it was not merit by which we were judged. The women are less feared.

Hence, when I entered the post college world, I saw a balance of men and women in those spaces but always more women, always more Whites; Mexican males depended on the site, especially since I entered the field of education.

By this time, I knew that females were given some preferential treatment. Not that I complained, I just accepted this fact as normal. Maybe it was part of my Mexican machismo that women should be given some preference. I had a caballero upbringing, but more important I was raised by a mother. I had a consciousness that the women should be treated better than the men because of my mother. Our mother is what we search for in a future woman; motherly like. In school, we were made more conscious of women, but I never learned any consciousness of us men to be. We were told to be kind to women, but I quickly learned that the females were not kind to us males. They were not being educated to be respectful of men, and I quickly learned that females were given preference and they could be cabronas at the same time. I began to comprehend the Rap fetish with the word "bitches" in their songs. Even though many rappers are harshly criticized for referring to women as 'bitches," to be honest, maybe they were just venting out their gender anger. As a man, I can honestly say that I have never met a woman who was not a bitch. And I do not make this judgment stereotypically, approach a woman and see how they first react. See how a woman reacts when she does not get her way and you will understand the Rappers anger. Men have to vent too.

And the most obvious power of women is that they choose who they want to mate with. All they have to do is wait, and the men arrive like zopilotes. Women attract vultures, but they choose which one. I would not change these rules though. I like the hunt, for it makes me feel testosterone even though I maybe rejected. Mexican women can marry out of the barrio as my wife stated even if they have to put up with vulgar dirty White men.

What bothers me though is the lack of recognition women have for their preferential treatment. On one hand, they benefit but simultaneously are quick to cry unfair treatment. In the work place, I see this exploitation and many of these women are eager to join Whites in their attack against men. Not that Chicano males do not, but women are just as culpable in this behavior and even worse, because they have sexual harassment protection. Whether true or not! My mother believes that women do not realize how much easier life is for women and women at home. Is any Chicana feminist going to counter this Mexicana of six decades of university life who had six children, five of whom are males? My mother is my guru.

Once in a conversation with three males and a female student, the male student named Efrain who works as a stockbroker mentioned that at ING, Mexican females were given promotions much faster than Mexican males. I had to stop and ask him, "Deberas you are a stockbroker." How many Mexican American stockbrokers do we know? And his best attribute is he believes in helping Raza; he had not sold out his identity to fit the White model. I met Efrain in Chicano Studies although an Economics major. His interest was there and the lure of money had not made him a Republican. A stockbroker Chicano, orale!

But as he elaborated that Mexican females not only were considered much more for promotional positions but that they also played the role. He stated apologetically that he felt they used their sexuality for their advancement. He clarified he was not generalizing or woman-hating, just observations from his work place. He further stated that some Chicanas had been promoted even though they had less experience or even less qualifications than him (I have seen this too). As a licensed broker, he had to pass examinations that he had studied a lot for, but because they kept pointing to his lack of a B.A., he was rejected for promotions. Plus, he was the primary breadwinner and had been for twelve years for his four younger siblings. As he stated, he put his life on hold for them. Even if not a father, Chicano males are expected to provide one way or the other for the family. That is an incredible burden: someone must always be sacrificed for others.

Then after Efrain stated his circumstance, one Chicana Roselyn began to raise her voice and complain; she stated the following: "I cannot believe you stated those sexist comments, Chicanas have been oppressed by comments like that." She was livid. One of those aggressive moments, but I felt I had to at least mention that because the beauty of a female body, there were certain preferences women received in comparison to men. Brown males have no cleavage or hips to flaunt. Mexican women do, including my mother, and based on this characteristic, why would they not. And Mexican females are gorgeous so why would they not have that slight advantage. Look at the novellas or television in English or Spanish.

I know women want to be known for their brains, but I do not want to be exploited for my body either. Because I do not have cleavage, I should not be ignored for a promotion and that is what Efrain argued. Roselyn was mad because the conversation continued into the class the following week. I was somewhat scared because of the sexist label, but I realized, if we cannot have this discussion, we should not be in higher education. Why is Mexicana preferential treatment not subject to debate, especially at the institutions of higher learning? Are universities now the modern Vaticans dictated by neo ten commandments: Thou shall not criticize: white women, Chicana, Gays, Lesbians, Joto Faggot communities, white women, Chicana, Gays, Lesbians, Joto Faggot communities and men who were dresses to the university.

How could we not criticize those fachas as my mother would state?

A third student, Adriel a Mexicano-Cubano (strange but they exist although he is more Mexican than Cuban on a certain cultural level), pronounced chingalo versus chingar. He stated a similar experience, and Roselyn was not only angry at one but at all three of us at the same time.

In the subsequent years, slowly the discussion has turned to the lack of Mexican male understanding. The most obvious reason due to the gender rights battles of the past was that Mexican males have the lowest college enrollments of any group in the country but also the highest manual labor rates —bracero work as Ruben Lopez calls it—plus the highest death rates by occupation. Every time a Mexican male goes to work, he faces the threat of death. Everyday a Mexican faces the threat of death by simply working for the family. Does UPS recruit women to move boxes? The US Army and UPS salivate at 18 year old Mexican American males for their testosterone. Sometimes that is the only option they have before a hernia, or a dislocated testicle injury sets in. Where women drafted for the Vietnam War as it occurred with my tio? When I filled out the selective service card at age 18, I was scared to submit it and to not submit it. If an American war occurred as they do every ten years, I was fregado and if I did not submit the card, I risked imprisonment. Do women have to face that fear?

If the Army or Marines did not devour you, UPS would with their last choice of employment. Remember the hernia or the endless insults from superiors who care less for the salvation of those testicles that carry the future. And if men do not hustle, they are lazy. Go home to your wife and we will see how quickly the love is over and the crisis of the marriage begins. Would a woman choose you in the first place without a job? As Ruben Lopez, the Filosofo del este de Los Angeles on Folsom Street, says, "Women do not look for a husband in the county general relief office." A Mexican male never truly wins. The endless question: did you get a job? My 30's have been endless and useless job searches.

The trend of more women in college is also visible for Mexicans. In the classes I teach, I generally average more women, and once I even had a winter session course where the 15 students were all females. I mentioned the gender imbalance and the women attacked me, but as I told them, I might be teaching, but my wife is at home enjoying January off while yo me la chingo. So I as the male in the class was nonetheless working. Those females could attend college from 11 am to 2 pm. I still need a permanent job.

Simply, Mexican males become breadwinners even before they turn 18, and the luxury of education in their mid twenties is just that, a privilege. If they have children, they definitely have to work whether separated or not. The Mexican male is even more of a ghost at the state universities, but nothing is done to remedy or at least to encourage them to attend. There has been talk about the near 60% female ratio, but that discussion takes hold in terms of White males but not Mexican Americans. Like we have national sympathy. White people want only to enslave us, and we only want stable employment, all for those tacos de carne asada. Our whole work is relegated to the philosophy of can I buy tacos whenever I want them?

Some might argue that Chicano males are well represented in the classroom as professors but only because they have to provide. How is that a privilege? I teach from Long Beach to San Fernando so the basics are met. Nobody is saying; let's give Julian an opportunity so he can survive. On the contrary, we are losing. In the spring of 2007 semester, a Chicana who had less experience than me was given a course even though I have more teaching experience all to make the department gender balance. I am an endless male body so fuck him.

The college argument for Mexicans is still within the outdated gender oppression model which to me seems too simplistic. All is fair in love and war. Who are we to judge our parent's marriage? I am against domestic violence, but I comprehend it. Sometimes my father was hard and soft as my mother was. Maybe he needed to be hard. On occasions, I feel I need to be a cabron, and in the college setting, the Chicanas in the places where I have taught need to be put in their place because they act imprudently.

I have taught at California State University, Long Beach, Dominguez Hills, Los Angeles, Loyola Marymount, East Los Angeles, Golden West, Glendale, and Mission College. At every location except for Mission, there has always been one problematic female colleague that even other females did not like.

I have learned from the universities that because of this preferential female treatment, they tolerate their childish behavior more. At Loyola Marymount, the former chair herself a female who retired did not invite the younger female to her after party because they never liked each other. The dean knew that many students did not like that young faculty member, but he put up with her even with endless complaints. The students liked me though and that was all I needed even if they did not rehire me. I hope I go to hell because if I have to see those Catholics hijos de su chingada madre, then I will really be encabronado at God.

At Cal State Los Angeles, the Chicano Studies department was in identity and gender crisis. They hired a Salvadorian to teach to Chicanos. Salvadorians and Chicanos have nothing in common. She mis-educates the students, and when they refute her, she complaints about the mistreatment and the intellectual challenge. We Mexicans have a culture; we do not need somebody else's imposition. But she is protected. Then they hired a Cornell graduate, who calls herself a postmorderniststructuralchicanafeminist who after some quarters does not have students enroll in her class. The college brings in their affirmative female action, and these women turn off other women. Where is the logic?

While at CSU Dominguez Hills, one former chair retired because he was sick but actually hired a female to replace him. This woman Eva was smart, but because she was humble. She would talk to me and treated me kindly. I wished she had become chair but the Black Dean Selassie Williams gave her a hard time when she requested a leave, so she quit and left to Redlands. I felt the department lost a good person, but she prioritized her daughters. She was human. She was a college professor, but a mother at the same time who shuffled schedules like any of us.

When Eva departed, only three or four men remained and we got along great. We had our own classes, talked when we had to. I was friendlier with an older man, kept my distance from the new young faculty, but we were cordial. When the Black dean rejected our hire and instead brought in a White woman, I left because it was all a façade. The Black dean did not want a strong Chicano male department. Black Studies feared our expansion, and he brought in a white woman apologist, who fired the acting secretary another Chicana, Eva Diaz. The new White chair, Irene Morris Vasquez fired Eva even though Eva was bilingual, simply because she was there before Irene arrived; she was terminated for being associated to us men. I was aware that the other men remained, but I had resigned out of protest for Irene's selection. Come on, Dominguez Hills has the reputation of being the ghettowhitetrash university of the CSU. Two good Chicanas were forced to leave by the Black dean, and the new White hire paid no respect to those there before.

At California State University, Long Beach, two Chicanas were hired. The one who left was low on social skills. She had been rude to a female student of mine and that should never have happened. People skills should always supersede any PhD. She apologized, but the damage was done and the college covered it up. The other faculty member is not friendly; nobody likes her and she pretends to be righteous. She is righteous and lazy at the same time. Yet the males are all terrified of her, so they never call her on issues. She can sit through a five hour meeting and never contribute to the discussion. And she is so pious, but the first to flaunt her cleavage as she did at a summer meeting where her breasts hung out. She would have made Janet Jackson seem innocent. However, she would be the first to complain if we stared too much even though we could not help ourselves because she was chairing the meeting.

Earlier, she was given time off because her ex companion died. Since when does one remember the ex other than to hate them? Finally, the males complained about doing too much that she was forced to do work. They as a department all believe they have written the greatest literary critique, but no one has published a book.

This is what I am complaining about: double standards. People pretend to hold me accountable for thinking, yet they act freely with no consequences. I have the negative reputation for being macho, but nobody has visited my classroom and my evaluations are excellent. A little profound thinking would do all us of some good, but Chicano heterosexual macho proud thought is rejected. When the men are alone, we can talk ideas and disagree but always agree together.

At the community colleges, it is the same. East Los Angeles is manipulated by the lone Greek female in Chicano Studies. This is how they kill our curriculum. When she was chair, she never hired a female. When a second female was hired, she was so problematic and arrogant with her skimpy outfits, she used East Los Angeles College as a springboard to another university. The Chicano males remained because they know racism would not hire them outside of East Los Angeles.

Tranquil normal Chicanas are hard to come by. Even the new females hired sense more hostility from the Greek female than the men. When a woman wants to complain about another woman, then there are problems.

I have sensed the same problem from other non-Mexican women too. Some White, some Latinas. White women will always be a problem for Mexican men because of the racial supremacy they carry and their Bunco mind set. Other Latinas that I have clashed with have been Puerto Ricans both at East Los Angeles and Golden West Colleges. I never really had conversations with them, but they worked the backstage to rid me and it worked. Maybe I am too Mexican and too macho, but those putas would never confront me because they do not have the courage, so they have to hide in the skirt of the law. Maybe the devil does wear a dress, but I view non-Mexican Latinas as instant enemies to Mexican females and males because they have been Americanized and, Americanization creates the fear monger of the Chicano and Chicana.

When it's only Chicano males with the same wave length, we have no trouble. We know our plan of action, survival. We know the enemy, White people and their surrogates. We know what we need to do. If we feel we need women, they will be hired but not at the expense of equality. I have recommended Chicanas who sometimes have been hired and other times plainly disregarded.

The problem with Chicana preferential treatment is that they divide us Mexicans from each other. This is my criticism. Chicanas do not look out for us Chicanos. When we protect ourselves, we are chauvinist.

My Berkeley friend, Marcos Ramos told me that his ex-friend was admitted to the University of Texas, Austin with a 3.4 grade point average while he was denied admission with a 3.7 grade point average. Both were Cal graduates, and he had advised her to enroll in some other courses to better her GPA.

His current girlfriend was admitted to graduate school with a 3.5 GPA and has completed her dissertation in psychology while he struggled to be admitted into graduate school in counseling at San Francisco State University. The majority of students are females.

Thus, the Chicano male with a higher grade point average was denied admission to graduate school, as Chicanas with lower scores were admitted and are soon to be doctors. He helped them both out financially, so his role of provider is still there while others progress at his expense.

Marcos' cousin from Tracy, Alejandro Peña, once mentioned his interest in comedy, maybe trying a little humor. As I bit into my taco de carne asada he stated:

"If there was space for Boy George, there must be room for me."

I almost choked from laughter, and until today, I laugh about his poignant comment: if there was space for a White immigrant man from England wearing a dress with make up, lip sticky todo, there has to be space for us Mexican American men. Right?

Chapter Eight

The Avoidance of Mexican Men
by Chicana Feminism

"The course on Chicana Feminism teaches us to disrespect males and almost,
but not quite, to hate them."

Crystal Alvarez
California State University, Long Beach Student

As my writings have emphasized a White created conflict imposed on both
Mexican males and females, the logical extension is to analyze what has been
permitted to be published in courses that focus on women.

When the Chicano era created an allure of openness and what had to be
studied, it seemed correct that women would be part of the study of Mexican
people as a whole. Racist oppression was both exercised on the men and the
women but through different forms. As my wife stated, "A Mexican barrio
male cannot marry up and out while a woman can." Obviously not all women
can and do make such choices to marry a man from another race, so it was
not universal.

Somehow and I am not quite sure how the argument was made, except
through the influence of White feminism, that the same logic used in White
feminism should be applied to study Mexican females. Of course, nobody in-
vited my mother or grandmothers to participate in the discussion, so their experience was left out. Not all women were included and those with families
were especially ignored. As a result what took hold was the villianization of
the Mexican male based on the White male model of domestic violence; the
same applied to Mexicans. Yet it seemed that Mexican males were more negatively stereotyped by the one characteristic that defined them, el macho.

Machismo has been associated to Mexican men only but not to other men
or women. Machismo seemed to explain the negative treatment of the women,

71

but nobody really discussed the positive or the negative attributes or purpose. Only Mexican men seemed to be stereotyped for domestic violence, but the behavior was also apparent in White and Black men. And women were not culpable in any of these behaviors; they could instigate but they were immune. It was as if their behavior had no consequences even if the result was abusive. As some Chicanas have gained access to positions of authority, the result has been the same as Whites in power. "The Mexican American women in power in the Los Angeles Community College District create problems for Chicano Males," an anonymous acquaintance stated.

Even today, Mexican American men are conscious of machismo to the point that they are apologetic of being male. The news segment especially in Spanish at times eggs the men in the machismo debate, and the reporters insist that machismo is a characteristic of Mexico not suitable for the modern US. But to stereotype Mexican men ignores the American reality of fighting. If a man does not fight, he will be walked over especially by women. Life does not favor men, check out the divorce courts. Mexican women chastise machismo because it does not favor them, so they downplay it. But as my mother taught me, "Cuidado con una mujer; beware of a woman." Women are not inocentes. I have concluded after years of male searching that I need to be macho; if not, a woman or anybody will walk all over me. I need to be macho for survival purposes because if a person is not fighting, defeated he will become. But the violence attributed is not machismo or Mexican-based only.

In a recent report, recent Mexican immigrant arrivals to Chicago demonstrated that they were more peaceful compared to Black or White males, but the rate of violence among second or third generation of Mexican Americans revealed that they had become more violent akin to American society. America forces Mexicans to become more violent, aggressive and unfriendly. When do we greet each other in Los Angeles? We do not practice the custumbres de buenos dias, buenas tardes, buenas noches? White people never greet us. We Mexicans are scared into what is right or wrong, and tragically we have followed White people. That is why Mexico is a much better place, people se saludan and that to me is a civil society.

Furthermore, the stereotype of Mexican men as wife beaters is too simplistic; I saw both. Some men did and others who did not. It was not uniform. I saw it as violence across the board. I heard the word safado or chisquiado, but we children got disciplined by beatings that depended on the severity of our misbehavior. My mother gave me some chingazos that I'll never forget, but she could because she was my mother. She spanked me because she loved me. And it was beyond spanking, era una chingiza, again depending on my misdeeds or her anger. She would tell us, "Les pego porque los quiero" y tomatelo the discipline came. Of course I was angry but never mad at her. She was my jefa. I had been raised to respect her and I did.

Even today, she claims those chingizas, the spankings were the reason none of us turned out as cholos. She might have a point, because we were loved and spanked simultaneously. She raised five Mexican males, none were cholos, although we had a blacksheep who was more of a prankster, but she never let up on him or gave up on him. She blamed his meningitis as a child. The other brothers were calm and at worst moody. All five of us completed high school; the youngest one was forced to attend adult school for one English class, once again, that damn subject, but he finished because she threatened to beat the shit out of him. And he respected her. Three of us are college graduates with mediocre jobs, but we have the faux titles, and the other two completed 30 units each of college. So all of us including my mother have had some college preparation.

None of us has ever been arrested and in Los Angeles, for a widowed Mexican mother to avoid high school dropouts and the cholo syndrome in the heart of the cocaine capital of the south bay—Lennox— was an accomplishment. She credits those belts for setting us straight. She mocks the recent defamation and police show of arresting the Cholos as more of a farce. They need love and chingazos, but the mother must be attending to them, not to other people who are making money off of her. She states, the Cholos want the media too, they can be movie stars and get attention they never received. How can they solve the Cholo question if most people do not know them? Buy them rines (rims) and they will behave.

Even today, she will ask my nephew proudly, "Recuerdas cuando te pegaba mijo; si ama." My mother is all proud she spanked mi sobrino Tony Perez who respects her by agreeing with her. My sister and I just laugh at my mother's ocurrencias. Maybe some spanking did us good and those marriages for good or bad were to be judged that way.

But machismo was not solely based on this; to be macho was to be male and ser hombre was difficult because we had to deal with women, work, White people and the stress of survival.

Yet, unfortunately, these aspects have not been studied because White women instantly criminalized machismo and Chicanas were not open to multiple interpretations or definitions. The curriculum instantly became: the male is evil, and it was easy to bedevil us because White feminism scorched males irregardless of racial oppression. White women were not oppressed as compared to Mexican males. And tragically, the universities wanted to be politically correct and like mandilones (apron wearers) that they were, women were allowed to dictate their new gender view. This occurred as long as Whiteness was maintained. And it has been. There are Women Centers but no Mexican American male centers. Maybe that is fine; we would not want the Chicano Male center to become a congregation site for the jotos as the Women's Center has become the lesbian axis at California State University, Long Beach.

Chicanas were able to also make the gender argument off the skirts of White women, but how was academia a participant in the Chicano Movement, when the Chicano Movements were situated in barrios or some work sites, not colleges? My grandmother and father, Luz and Julian, were engaged in farmworker work stoppages from the mid 1960's-1969. Academia did not talk to Luz; they did not ask her about her participation. Yet the drive for an expanded curriculum would be divided by this gender and later gay claims. Everybody's story wanted to be told. As they planned to do so, self interest and lifestyles took hold because the colleges were made up of many of these people. The only work places I have seen men wear dresses are at universities and Catholic Churches.

The Anglo Saxon curriculum was expanded to include women, gays (look at the Republican Party Joto scandals; faggot but still racially conservative) Blacks, Asians and Chicano Studies but as long as the men were de-emphasized.

Chicana academicians coined themselves with no self creativity into feminism. Their feminism was based on the White female model. But the field of Chicano Studies was to be about Mexican people that included both men, women, children, brothers and sisters, ancianos y ancianas (old folks). It was about resurrecting the Mexican identity from that of a negative meaning to its rightful cultural significance based on history, cultura and upbringing. Yet Chicana feminists complained that they were specifically excluded and they used the male chauvinistic attitude of Chicano movement leaders to mentally right their splinter. I doubt these male leaders wanted to be fighting in the front fearing a violent power structure. The conditions lent themselves and they went forward.

Mexican male leaders have arisen from time past, but since the US invasion of Mexico, males were always fighting the White upfront from Joaquin Murrietta to Geronimo to our jefes. They were protecting women, children, and the land. The 1960-1970's were just new versions of generational Mexican struggles. The women wanted the limelight too but did not want to be soldiers. Being a soldier means following orders and not disobeying. I never remember Coretta Scott wanting to stand and lead the marches. She was taking care of her children. Why? Because that was her duty to protect them and raise them. The duty of King led to his assassination or hunger strikes by Chavez or court preparation by the Brown Buffalo. The father protects the family as a whole: the mother specifically protects the children and guides the man. These are native roles long forgotten. How is this male chauvinistic? The Brown Buffalo and King died, Chavez starved himself on occasions, how were they mistreating women, they sacrificed dearly. They imposed decisions over other males too. In certain circles, Chavez was a tyrant to other men.

And by Chicanas insisting on wanting to be leaders, they attacked the man's manhood. Not only can women choose what man they want and when they want him, they now wanted to be their boss too. And of course the notion of White male disrespect was there because they too judged Mexican males as not acting male enough. Those specific feminists insulted the position and respect of men, and in the classroom they took out their antipathy. Chicana academicians act like they did a lot, but if they were attending college, how were they participating in work stoppages the way my grandmother Luz or father Julian did? Quietly with no fanfare or documentaries with solely believing these risks would get them paid better to improve their lives.

Why did Chicana feminists not protest and organize women against attending any form of misa-mass because the Catholic Church tells them, women cannot be priests, but every Sunday the majority of those in attendance are Mexicana women singing La Guadalupana, la Guadalupana. Mexicana women would have kicked their culos for interfering in the sanctity of their thoughts and beliefs. If Chicana feminists were truthful to ending oppression, they would have begun with the dogma of Catholicism that has many Mexicans in mental shackles.

The curriculum as it now stands by these feminists entirely ignores Mexican males even if they were raised by single or widowed mothers. My Salvadorian friend Marvin Martinez once stated: "We always hear about the Black single mother head of household, but Mexican American women are entirely ignored like your mother who raised five males as a widow." Mi jefa es spectacular, but she will never be recognized because she does not fit the Chicana feminist standard. First because she does not have a doctoral degree, second, because she is one of many Mexican American faces simply ignored, third, because she is not a lesbian, fourth, she is not a movie star and lastly, she had too many children.

What's even more alarming is Chicanas have entirely missed the point in many curriculum factors vital to the comprehension of Mexican people. Chicana feminists never talk about Mexican culture being matriarchal. They write from a patriarchal Catholic point of view and ignore the power of mothers, both good and bad but also their traditions as madres. They ignore the knowledge of the mother as a teacher. The more Americanized, the less respect they have for their mothers. My sister-in-law would rather read White books on childbirth than listen to the mother who gave birth and raised her. She recently stated she wants to send her son to a Christian school to learn Spanish, but when mentioned by her sister to have their mother teach him, she scoffed. How disrespectful except when she wants her handout. For that mentality, she needed a beating. I am disgusted by her notion of superiority over my Apache mother-in-law. This is a White product.

Chicana feminists have excluded the kitchen. The stove is the altar. Mexican civilizations have been transmitted in the kitchen, from generation to generation, but feminists have portrayed the kitchen as a prison. The word cocina summarizes my childhood memories with my mother at the altar. Nothing satisfies me more than a simple plato de frijoles con tortillas de harina y papas con huevo. If I had to choose between an expensive dinner or my mother's touch, chale, los frijoles win out. My mother judges a woman by her ability to cook, si no sabe cocinar para que quieres una mantenida. What good is a woman who only freeloads!

Chicana feminists have also rebuked birth. Natural childbirth in the late 20th century has been replenishing the genocide of Mexicans from the 1850-1880's in the deserts of Northern Mexico. Mexicans are now at 30 million and counting in the US and those feminists have imposed the White shame of too many children all for the ideal notion of it's my body. It is not your body; it belongs to the group because group survival should be more important. Did Chicano males have a right to make that claim during the draft or when I had to register for the selective service? My body belongs to everybody but me and yet women want to have that special privilege.

My friend Rosalinda Moran Moctezuma dropped out of the Master's program in Chicano Studies at California State University, Northridge because a female professor named Juana Mora told her she had to choose between her 14 year old son or school. Rosa quit school and later enrolled at CSU Los Angeles, but the bitter experience will always linger in her. Que viva la mujer while they screw other women with children. For that, she deserves a beating.

In reference to childbirth, there is nothing more hurtful than to see a woman linger over not having a baby. I should know, I lived it. These feminists play God and ignore the power of motherhood. In Mexican culture they are called solteronas y amargadas. What good is a woman who did not have a child? Motherhood knows no gender differences, but they have specific roles designed for the boys and girls. Mothers generally love their males and females, but as jefas are humans, they sometimes fail there. They are human afterall.

Chicana feminists further avoid the fact that men die younger than women do. How can any woman neglect the point that the opposite sex dies before her on average. Sometimes the reality of life is more potent than any other force that I feel I have intentionally been led by the hand of Usen, the Apache mother of the valleys and mountains to make these arguments. In my family, all the men have died younger except for my paternal grandfather. My father Julian, tio Pocaluz and tio Cuco all died under 40. Cuco died at 24, Julian at 30 and Pocaluz at 38. Natural or work related.

My Nina Kika died before my Nino Gus (my father's parents), but she was eight years older than mi Nino and still my father died before she did. When my mother's father died in 2002, Miapa Matiaz nonetheless died before Miama Alberta. I remember my brother Mario Alberto state after the funeral, "Once again, the men die first." Where is the attempt to understand? Who knows maybe I am next? Women take us for granted just like White people do. Vayanse a la chingada!

In early 2006, the last of my patriarchs died, mi Nino Gus, my grandfather. There were no other children (Gus and Kika adopted my father and all of us), he was my father figure after my father died. My father's biological mother lives in the Imperial Valley, but we have all lost touch with the clan. We would not recognize each other if we met on the streets. With the passing of Nino, I became the elder at age 37. At such a young age, I am expected to have wisdom because there are no older male figures even on my mother's side. In all fairness to my Nino, he hung around to see all of us five males as adults. His death was like reliving my father's death; my only consolation was that he was reunited with my father. They really cared for each other, and I saw the powerful bond between men that has nothing to do with sex or interest, just cuates, carnales who lived life to the fullest. I had to let my Nino go, but I cried in anger for my father's loss. Until today, I have not been able to visit his grave. His muerte cemented that fact that I was permanently orphaned from male figures, but fortunately I have my mother.

Six months later, my father-in-law Theodorus "Ted" Aartman succumbed to lymphoma after a ten year bout with this cancer and endless cycles of toxification of his body. We saw him literally stop breathing as he fought to survive and never accepted the fact his life was over. Once again, I was burying another male figure. Another male death! Explain to me how I rationalize my gender falling like flies. Explain to me how I rationalize to my wife that her father is dead at her young age of 36 and his young age of 66. How do I comprehend that I have seen more males in coffins and have served as pall-bearers for many of the? But true Chicanas care for them as I saw my mother-in-law, my wife's tia Armida and my mother Monica worry about this Dutch immigrant who was adopted into Mexican matriarchy. They suffered just as much to see him suffer. True Mexican mothers care for their men until their death even if not their sons or husbands. Once again, for my carnal Ruben and I, we lost a father figure even if he was hard to handle. He would sit and talk to us like men and even adopted our lingo. He loved the word "loco."

In September, three months after Ted died and nine months after Nino died, my mother's ex boyfriend Ramon "Monchis" Guerrero died at the age of 57. We knew he was sick just as Ted or Nino were, but we always hoped he could survive. He died at age 57. Monchis was my step-father even though they never married by paper. He was there even when I did not want him there. He never turned his back even when I did. That is love for a son that never was his. He stuck it out and I am sorry. I moped about my own father, but when another appeared and he wanted to be, I was not receptive. Yet he fed me hamburgers at times when my mother could not. His love was a verb and I did not know how to appreciate him. For this, I am an asshole, but I honor him by crying to him and writing to not forget his memory. He was at my high school graduation; he taught me some mechanics, fought to defend us, and cried for my uncle Pocaluz in a howl I never knew existed, but I should not have been surprised as he was Apachis too from Calexico (his family were from Cananea in Sonora). Monchis was a surrogate father who wanted to marry my mother. For my younger brother, Jorge, he was the only father he knew.

When I was told Monchis died, I felt angry at life. He had moved on, my mother and he parted ways. He had remarried and the lady wanted nobody around. I respected that, but Monchis was still special. He died sad, and the crazy wife did not even have a funeral. There was no velorio for flowers, rosario or misa. I could not even attend the entierro because I was fighting for a second class, and at that exact moment of 11 AM, he was being returned to Usen and Guadalupe, was my first day of work. And yet even in fucking death, the priest was late. I do not even know where Monchis is located in Holy Cross where all my Inglewood rancheria people are buried at. I felt triste for my younger brother Jorge, for Monchis was the only father he had. Monchis probably spoiled him, but he attended his baseball games and paid attention to him when I did not or could not because of life. I felt for Jorge, for he never knew his father Julian and now at age 27, his father had died. My mother said he cried endlessly. Had my mother married Monchis, she would have been widowed twice. I do not know what was worse, their break up ten years ago or her attending his burial. At least in the break up, she gave him his freedom.

Monchis' mother Doña Adela has buried three of her sons. Monchis older brothers Jesus and Jose (Gavacho), died in 1980 and 1984. How does she survive?

In between these deaths, I have also buried three males I grew up with. Two cousins, a childhood friend, my friend Fernando, and mi primo Antonio (both died of heroin overdose). Americanization somehow forced them there. Both were from Inglewood. Antonio became a cholo, but he was not as a child, so what happened? He endured a blade across his face and endless fights as a member of Inglewood 13, but I played with Tony as children. He was not a cholo then. Where is his understanding and his mother's endless pain? Belen was my grandfather Nino's roommate at the time of his death. Tragically, Tony died in an Inglewood alley, north of Florence at the young age of 27.

Fernando died five years later at age 31 also of heroin overdose in Hawthorne. Fernando was economically stable because his father was a police officer, but somehow the White enclave drove him back to his grandmother's home in Hawthorne. And just like that two childhood brothers were dead. A few years later, my other cousin Antonio from Mexicali also died but of AIDS. Still, I have never been to a funeral of a young woman who I knew from my childhood or as an adult. We Mexican men are at greater threat of dying. Does anybody care?

How does feminism console the motherly pain of Belen, Genobeva, Linda, Doña Adela, Luz Maria, Alberta and many jefitas-mothers who have lost sons to life? My mother Luz, my father's biological mother, has buried two sons. In 2003, my father's brother, comic-tecato-farmworker-San Quentin release for self defense, Jose was killed by a reckless 16-year-old female driver in Mexicali as he stood on the porch socializing outside. The car pinned him and crushed him against the house. After two weeks of agonizing and suffering, he died. My grandmother Luz accepted the fact that death was his salvation. I see the anguish in her Apache face. He had lost his residency from the Clinton amalgation of past crimes and was a drug user because he worked for thirty years bending to pick lettuce to survive the pain and feed White women's ever quest of dicting. He was repaid by losing his residency, and instead of sitting in jail to fight the case, he renounced his American card and instead accepted death. My abuela accepted death as his salvation from hell. She has never mentioned him, and I know she yearns for death, but Usen has not called her. As she once stated to me in my early 20's, there is nothing more painful than the loss of a son or daughter by a mother. She has taught me more about life than any university. I write in her honor, for her name Luz, Light is my vision.

My brother David once suffered an accident upon returning from work. He fell asleep at the wheel from the endless hours of work for survival, so his wife and child could eat. Even today, he works eighty hour weeks in the summer time in eastern Oklahoma for a road company. Sure, my sister-in-law gave birth, but he has to maintain them or he is a bad father.

I might die from all the freeway flying I do. And yet, Usen tells me that only my mother will ever love me unconditionally, to not expect much from strangers.

Tragically Paulo Friere, a Brazilian, is utilized more as a methodology for understanding Mexican cultural education when our true source should be our mothers. As my wife states, Mexicans are already literate in the oral tradition and rich in culture because of our mother. Three idiotic imposed books from outsiders do not make us literate.

Chicano males in academia now walk around feministas as if on eggshells and are really intimidated by them. The fear of the macho label or sexual harassment has men angry, but few dare to challenge this warped paradigm. I am categorized as too macho because I state that three courses on the Chicana and no course on males is wrong. I am ignored, but they have read my complaints or because I stated that certain jobs are only made for women while Chicano males are still expected to be cutting the grass or digging ditches for less pay than that woman who works as an undergraduate advisor. I have never seen women standing in front of Home Depot waiting as day laborers. How is that gender equitable?

The quote in the beginning of the chapter was a commentary made to me by this superb student who really comprehended that Mexicans must stand as men and women collectively and not as individuals led by White female perversions. Furthermore, Crystal could not accept the derogatory perspective of males because her father had been a positive person who always taught her to be proud of being Mexican. Miapa Matiaz, my mother's father, was similar to Crystal's father; he was always kind to his daughter, my mother, and I was fortunate to have witnessed that. I really miss his presence, I can imagine my mother's pain for her father. Where is the understanding of males and females interacting as one?

Chapter Nine

Mexican Immigrants Preferred Over Mexicoamericanos

"Chicanos are lazy."

Guillermo Esqueda

"Los Jarochos son flojos, no son trabajadores como los del norte."

Ramon "Monchis"
Mexicali Native; Lived in Lynwood;
Relocated to Veracruz, Veracruz

"Me gusta como canta Lupillo Rivera porque fue el primer Mexicano de Los Angeles en cantar en el Universal Amphitheater."

Monica Camacho, Mi Jefa

A special thank you to my wife for inspiring and encouraging me to write on this difficult topic.

In 2000, I attended the Chicano Graduation at UC Berkeley to watch my carnal's graduation. I was honored that my cuate asked me to go to his graduation in that hideous setting of Berkeley. The city of Berkeley rubs me the wrong way. I cannot pinpoint the reason, but there are many: faux righteousness, progressives for Whites only, trapped northern Mexican history, dirty, run down housing and ransom rents. In an odd way, I still feel the dead Mexican souls in the Bay Area, so I tend to shy away. You cannot get more American Anglo Saxon Protestant Manifest Destiny Animus Americana than Berkeley and all roads lead to the university.

Although gladly I attended my cuate's graduation, it was more hype than reality. The Chicanos were no different; they engaged in the hype-mental masturbation and ego inflation of having graduated from "Cal" (means limestone in Mexican). Mi carnal Marcos Ramos somehow had not allowed himself to be coaxed by those ruffles and feathers. Even the faculty guest speaker, Pedro Noguera, an educational specialist advised them to be humble. "Always stay humble, because when in need humbleness will lift you up," he said.

Yet the most intriguing part of the ceremony were the two speeches given by two Chicanas. Both of these Chicanas gave discourses with the message aimed at one for being Mexican American, the other for being Mexicana. The Mexican American provided more of a class analysis, the Mexicana who read her speech in Spanish with that slight Chicana accent. The Mexican American stated that she should not be judged for her slight class advantage, the Mexicana stated that there should not be a class division but to recognize her harsh upbringing, the no papeles syndrome yet competent. I felt the tension in both their speeches. I thought, ah cabron, se estan dando verbal chingazos like the Black Rappers do it. I thought the shooting is next. It left me uneasy.

Seven years later, I am still attempting to make sense of this event. What had taken place continues a long and subtle battle between Northern and Centro Mexicans, both of whom have been shaped by the great American white border divide. This divide continues to haunt us, but generally most Mexican Americans and Mexican nationals live next door to each other in the same barrio and sometimes in the same house.

Mexican migration is extremely complex for many reasons. Many come for work, but that is no different than the European, Asian, Centro American or East Coast Americans who move to Califas for money. Everybody is allowed to come and exploit our lands. We Mexican Americans are the only native people to California even if first generation because we are geographical births by blood and land, yet Native California Mexicans are excluded. I do not want to spend an eternity on immigration from one side of the desert to the other side, but can you really immigrate in the same desert and ecological zone? Mexican nationals do not immigrate the way other people do; they just traverse the different Mexican landscapes.

Mexican national immigration consist mainly of working poor, but many are also professionals, college educated, business people and even millionaires. The Salma Hayeks (not Mexican; father is Lebanese); the Alejandro Gonzalez Iñarritu (movie director—not your regular Mexicano from the pueblos or ranchos) or the new heir of Jumex who lives in Beverly Hills and is showcased as a respectable figure in the White arts community but not in the Mexican American world of forgotten Estrada Courts muralists like Norma Montoya. Even my Nino's niece, Judith Magaña from Jacona who inherited land and leases it drives around in a Mercedes Benz, yet she lives in

Huntington Park with her Chapulin Colorado husband as my grandfather called him. And he has a Harley. He represents these Republican Mexican nationals who solely want a buck with no consciousness. I even once met a heart surgeon from Guadalajara who made a living from refereeing soccer games. Was he humbled?

However, because the US has done a near perfect superb historical lobotomy and Mexican nationals from the south have more or less accepted the fact that the northern halves of Sonora and Baja California are now Arizona and California, US lands, the notion of Northern Mexico ends at San Ysidro or Calexico even though that is a White imposed line. In Los Angeles, the people still call the region southern California which still connotates Baja or lower. I love the term Baja California. It is the name of my mother, how could I neglect her.

Still, because many people who have moved north from Centro Mexico where the region is not as desert intense as Sonora, there is sense that they are moving to a different country because for them, their definition of Mexico is their landscape. And vice versa, for us Mexicoamericanos, our definition of Mexico is solely desert and was I in culture shock to see green Mexico with no chamizos or nopales. Because of the geographical variation that exists in Mexico, I see central southern Mexicans culturally different because of that geography versus thinking of them as entirely different national citizens. I judge them culturally and they define me culturally too.

One time, this senor who was selling carpets with his beautiful sombrero looked at me and stated: "Usted parace que es de Sonora." The man was from Jalisco. We had this conversation in Whittier. I mentioned to him that I was and what he told me was that he judged me culturally as a Yaki. Listen, I can tell a Oaxaqueño or a Yucateco or a Michoacano based on appearance. I do not like the Jalisco people who pretend to be snobby though. They all pretend to come from Guadalajara when most come from small pueblos or ranchos.

At a certain point, the perception of all Chicanos looking Apache-Indian is very much based on the ethnic desert appearance of Mexicans born in el norte on either side of the airport. When I visit Mexicali, I look like the Cachanillas. When I am in East Los Angeles, I look Chicano (an East Los Angeles identity). When I was in Zuni, the people looked Mexican Apache to me. I could not tell the difference between them and my East Los Angeles College students. I even had a Hopi student—Kevin Polikemtewa— in my gang class once, and he told me that in Los Angeles everybody assumes he is Mexican. He looked like my cousins. He stated he was after all, but when I first met him, I asked him why he was interested in a course on Cholos, and he explained: "When the Hopi kids move to Phoenix and return to the reservation, they come back as Cholos; we have a Cholo problem on the reservation." You cannot get more Chicano than this.

Kevin and I had a similar height 6'5, similar brown color and similar facial structure which looks norteño, not from centro Mexico. When the man from Jalisco mentioned to me that I looked Sonorense, that is what he was stating. I have a straight Yaki Apache norteño look. Once I was wearing a blue bandana around my maseta with my long black hair and when my mother-in-law, another Apache saw me, she asked me sarcastically; "Are you on the war path?" I was honored by her observation. That is my ethnic Mexican look. Most people ask me first if I am Native American before Mexican. I say both, Northern Mexicans are native to the desert irregardless of White papers. My grandparents lived in a casa de adobe. I spent my summers in Mexicali in between the vulcan El Cerro Prieto that turned out to be red and the Sierra Cucapah and yet I was a US citizen.

Guillermo Esqueda (Don Memo) who is also from Guadalajara calls me as part of the Yakiada. He says his grandmother was an Adelita, a female soldier under the Mexican Revolution who fought with all sides for survival from Pancho Villas to the Federales. She would explain that she feared the Yakiada more than anybody else. They were the most savage. She was also native but from Xalisco-Huichol and if you see Don Memo, he is dark but has a different Mexican ethnic look. He picks on my family because he knows us all and calls us the Yakiada, but he is also conscious because he tells me, "You come from people who have suffered greatly; los indios del norte han sufrido mucho y se ve en usted y su mama."

Don Memo is an extremely educated man and knows the tragedy of Mexican history. He tells me, "Your people have suffered a lot." He cannot figure out why I am so Mexican-proud but admires it because the great geographical divide from centro Mexico is to think of Northern Mexicans as not really Mexicans, but more Indios. The soccer team in Cd. Juarez is called Los Indios; the logo is a soccer ball with a bandana wrapped around the ball. I laughed when I saw it because I realized that centro Mexicanos consider norteños, Indios first before Mexicans. They almost do not consider us Mexicans, not quite Mexicanos, especially those who have never traveled to Sonora or Baja California. And they let you know.

Once I met a Chicano anthropology student, Enrique, who was interested in Sonora-Baja California Mexicans and even though his family was from Mexicali via Jalisco, he saw himself more Jalisco. He had the look too, fair skin, green eyes with that eagle nose. He had what I call the "Los Altos look" a mountainous region of Jalisco-Leon Guanajuato look. I see this in my mother's side of the clan because my great-grandparents were from San Francisco del Rincon and had the same ethnic fair skin eagle nose look. My Nino Gus had this same profile. My mother was born and raised in the Imperial Valley, so the idea of being from Guanajuato is foreign to her. Any mention to that heritage insults her because she was born in Baja California. She is Baja California and rightfully so, she was born and raised there. The geography made her Apache. We are not like Americans who after three generations still call themselves Irish or Germans when the people back in Ireland or Deustchland do not consider them Irish or German.

Enrique mentioned how the Sonorense-Baja California Mexicans were extremely different, and he pinpointed to the fact that these people had no earlobes, that their earlobes were attached to their face. I laughed because my father and uncle Miguel were the same way and so am I. On my tio Miguel it almost seemed that the ear was attached from the middle of his cheek and stretched down towards his jaw. I laughed because I told Enrique like this as I pointed to my ear. He just looked at me in amazement. For all Mexicans, ethnic appearance, culture and accents are ways that we distinguish from each other. I had a student say in one of my classes that we Mexicoamericanos were different because we made our tamales from corn, not banana leafs. I laughed but thought, he is correct. These southern Mexicanos want to impose different habits we northern Mexicans know nothing of. I even get offended when I hear that Baja California is now referred to as Oaxacalifornia because of new Oaxaca people migrations. Ni madre, do not erase my Baja California name because you are threatening my identity. Who do you think you are? Respect the historical names. As my mother always says, everybody protects its own.

Even linguistically speaking, I grew up with Mexican lingua that was more Baja California than even Sonora. I know two different words in my Mexican Nahuatl version of Cachanilla because I grew up knowing I had to know the differences. It was even worse when I would meet centro Mexicanos, and they spoke their version of Mexican. I was always lost, I thought, ah cabron no se lo que dicen only to have other Mexicans who comprehended both clarify. A listing of my lingua: bichi, apapuche, cochise, guajolote, pata, cachanilla, chamizo, apapachar, casar, mesquite, machaca, chamaco, chamaca, Chicano, platano. These words mean encuerado, en espalda, puerco, pavo, pies, muchacho, muchacha, banana, in Mexican Spanish which is another form of Nahuatl. The words mean naked; piggyback, pigs, turkeys, foot, no translation for plant, shredded beef, kid-male, female, US Mexican and banana. If you throw Purepecha lingo, I understand zero. Even the names are different; they end with "cuaro" which seems to mean land as tlan means the same in Jalisco-Zacatecas. For us northern Apaches, the word "Chis" means land which is why the word Chi-cano is in use. Hopis, Mochis, Chis, Apachis, Comanchis and many other words. It is very complex, but we Mexicans know these varieties because we are cultured people. Culture is how we mark differences, which is why we do not identify with Centro Americans because they are too culturally foreign even if they seem to have a similar look.

Beyond centro Mexicans, there are even greater differences between Mexicoamericanos and Latinamericanos. Salvadorians have round pancake faces with beaky noses, Nicaraguanses look like they are in between Black and light black. Hondurans are a cross of all those people while Guatemalans are the closest to Mexicans but the culture throws everything off. It is too foreign for me. Even among Mexicans, my closest cuates are Apache Mexicans not people from Zacatecas or Jalisco. Those Zacatecano clubs are too different for me and me for them too. Now, if they become Baja California or Chicanoized, I can relate more. I recently had my vehicle fixed, and the vato was cool, as we talked he mentioned to me that he had learned his trait in Jalisco but moved to the east side. He told me what he enjoyed the most about Los Angeles were the tacos de carne asada. Carne Asada is not popular in Jalisco, but in California it is because it is Apache cultural food along with the burrito de carne asada. Ese vato was a todo dar. Not like those Jalisco purists who own the restaurant La Casita Mexicana in Bell and bash Los Angeles Mexican food as not authentic. They impose their Jalisco style food because that is all they know, but we do not eat soupy shredded beef, it has to be asada, barbecue with the flame hitting the meat. Nobody wants to recognize Mexican Los Angeles as Apache culture.

Music wise, it's the same, centro Mexico music is guitarra, more string ensemble without the drum. Norteño music is more drum whether the snare or the tambor, the big drum plus wind instruments. The native music of California is Banda Sinaloence with all wind instruments. When I hear this music, my heart rate accelerates. I love it. When I was a kid, we used to dance to Banda Sinaloence and hummed the songs because nobody sang them. When I read up on the music style of the Apaches, it was drum, wind, and hummed. We all knew the song, and we collectively hummed. I still do. The Norteño music with the sombrero is within the same style and the ever beautiful accordion. In centro Mexico, they do not really like Norteño music though as I learned in el D.F. Recently, it has become in style right. Maybe the north is winning them over because without doubt, the north is the heart of Mexico. Naco means heart, there is a border city in Sonora called Naco. In el D.F., Naco means low class but there is still heart.

The same could be stated about the love of the bullfights which could be akin to the running of the buffalo. Norteño music of the corrido is northern. At a corrido exhibit in San Diego, there was a corrido about a Kansas man who cried because there was no more Buffalo to hunt, celebrate and partake in nature. Evil Whites killed our traditions and the Buffalo was part of us too. It still is even if in our imagination and soul. I love the Buffalo. Oscar Zeta Acosta was correct.

The second definition besides geographical by way that Mexicans differentiate among each other is socialization. This new socialization is based on

Estados Unidos. Birth in the US makes Mexicans pochos, Chicanos, Mexicoamericanos. These are all really euphemisms for Americans and not Mexican. There is a clean divide. If born south of La Linea, Mexicano, if born north, American citizen. This one is more complicated because it is cooperation between White Americans and centro Mexicans on the fate of the north. How do outsiders from both sides determine what is Mexican or not?

He alli el detalle. The details are complex. American socialization is extremely problematic because the Americans have been changing or attempting to change Mexicans to Americans, yet racism through barrios tells the real picture. Americans have never accepted Mexicans and they never will unless they benefit from them. Do not let the lure of Antonio Villaraigosa interpret success. White people need a cheerleader and the mayor is an excellent choice even with his progressive stand. Structural change will never be permitted. Developers own Los Angeles. The advancement of one Mexican were developers and unions benefit, yet the majority of Chicanos in East Los Angeles still suffer from basic under-employment and half of the population lives in converted garages along crowded streets.

The educational socialization of Mexican Americans creates a permanent divide that centro Mexicanos will never comprehend just as they never understood why Mexicans in Los Angeles adopted the word Chicano. Most centro Mexicanos believe the adoption of Chicano means rejecting Mexicano while for Los Angeles Mexicanos, the word Chicano means becoming more Mexican, but more like the Mexicas who left Aztlan in search of the symbol of water: the eagle devouring the serpent. Centro Mexicanos do not comprehend this identity process and really chastise US Mexicans. The centro Mexicanos see this as a rejection of being Mexican and the ultimate result of Americanization, but they do not understand Apache culture. The word is a term of endearment much like many people referred to Mexicali as Chicali. The Chi in the desert people, but because Chilangos do not know a Baja California they could not see. Truth of the matter is, they have never cared about Mexicans north of the border. We are forgotten. The secretaria de educacion does not consider Mexicoamericanos for study beyond some abstract program that few people have heard of, much less citizenship.

All that centro Mexicanos see is that the Mexicanos from Los Angeles speak Spanish with a gringo accent, forgetting Spanish all together, looking down upon Tijuana and Mexico overall, not liking the cultural tradition, being embarrassed of their parents look and manual labor and all of a sudden having new names that are comical because how could Chicanos adopt American names. The biggest gripe is that US Mexicans are embarrassed for being Mexicano. In a certain way, they are correct, but the socialization must be understood.

My former student Don Memo who was a political PRI activist has made the comment "Chicanos are lazy" not to insult but to stir and inspire. He has on occasions stated that Chicanos are lazy because they have become too American and expect to have the same rights as Whites. He believes this has created a negative dependence on outsiders and institutions versus having the huevos to move on and fly from tree to tree much like a woodpecker does. Don Memo speaks from truth and experience. He explains that creative survival is what has led him to endure. He never knew hunger until he began to live in Los Angeles. He was not middle class in Guadalajara but educated, a reporter at age 18, a minor league Atlas soccer player, a political activist who fled for his life. He stated, "Vine a cayer al mentado oye del este de Los Angeles despues de haber estado con los negros." After living through the Black wars between United Slaves and the Panthers west of downtown Los Angeles, the East Side attracted him like a magnet.

When he first arrived to Los Angeles in 1975 and he had visited before as a tourist, he stated there were few Mexicans and they were not friendly. So he hung out with the Blacks. He was just as dark, and with his hair long, he could fit. He says his best attribute was his dancing, so he lived life as a brother. His jive is hilarious. Amazingly hilarious, but he lived among Blacks.

After moving to the hole in East Los Angeles, he realized the Chicanos were a negative version of Mexicans because of their Americanization. He ended up in not just East Los Angeles, but the pit of the east side, El Oyo, the hole where Obregon Park is located, in between Cholos and Cholos. And as an outsider, he was an easy target. James Diego Vigil has pinpointed that Cholos would easily target recent arrivals from south of the border. Quite frequently, they robbed and fought them. It is no coincidence, other Cholos were created as self defense mechanism. The US Cholos also referred to the newly created clicas as wetbacks. It was the worse Mexican nightmare to happen. Mexicans by birth or socialized Americans were committing most of the violence towards those who had arrived from south of the border. White people were channeling their racism and actions through the mouth of other Mexicans. So Don Memo fought cholo after cholo for survival. He stated it seemed like an eternity, and because Don Memo knew some boxing moves and had been a political activist in the early 1970's, he knew how to fight chavalos from the streets. He had fought soldiers and police in Mexico.

Eventually Don Memo became friends with them and realized that not only were they vasca, spit, they were also poor, neglected, unwanted, unaccepted, trouble makers and what he saw was a tragic affair of Mexican American life that he did not know existed. He saw them as the sons of the Bracero Mexicans who were the ranchero class from Mexico who were contracted to work in the fields of the US because their limited educational experience. They were now the fruit product of the vast movement of farm people who left centro Mexico with no education and lived day to day with no goals or aspirations.

At first I thought, que cabron. I still do not agree entirely with him because the Braceros were hard workers, but in Don Memo's eyes their hard work blinded them from the necessary education all needed. He felt that the hard work ethic neglected education. And in that aspect, Don Memo was not necessarily wrong. I was raised with the notion that Mexicans would rather send their children to hard labor before study, but my mother disproved such theory. The failure of Chicanos was based on the parents not society; the US wiped its hands clean of Mexican American obligation.

What Don Memo never quite understood until after three decades of life in the US was institutional racism that never included Mexicans. And yet he still does not quite comprehend this American fact but is more accepting of major limitations being imposed through new requirements for college transfer or the intentional tracking of Chicanos into basic English courses when they should be in college prep courses. He complains from this standpoint: "Do not let faux materialism consume you, study and prepare yourself and fight for this." When he mentions Chicanos are lazy, that is what he refers to: the settling of crimes through debt.

Since Don Memo studied medicine for one year, he has a thorough knowledge of biology and math. I met him at East Los Angeles College, and we are the best of friends. I think of him as my elder because he advises me and thinks I am super intelligent. He believes students should model me which I do not like because everybody must follow his own path. He also tells me that my love of Mexico and Mexicans is unique. I have a rancho tribal definition of Mexicans, and he likes that I lecture without books. He believes faculty must have their individual knowledge based on life not reading phrases from a book others have written. If you know your material you will not need a book. He is extremely smart even if he is also abrasive. But Don Memo's problem is that he does not have patience for Chicanos. And this turns off many especially my Chicano friend Ruben. They both think the same but their approaches are different.

What Don Memo fails to comprehend (but he's learned through his daughters) is the negative American socialization of Mexicans in schools. He fails to comprehend the effects of Anglo educational socialization even though he sees it. Most Mexico-born Mexicans, (Mexico born meaning two hundred miles past the border), have never lived the denial, the neglect of Mexican language and culture, the racism, the hatred and the contempt in California American society where the children know that the word Mexican means nigger. He grew up in Guadalajara 1200 miles away where the US is more of a dream, an illusion. He was not raised with police or border harassment;

American poverty which is shameful; under the notion that the word Mexican was dirty; or under border conditions where in Mexicali, if you spoke English the people looked down upon you and right across the border your cousins thought they were better off because they spoke English. He was not raised with his homeland divided in two. He grew up culturally in tact where Mexican traditions were something to be proud of and there were Mexican faces of many types.

In Guadalajara, a Mexican could be working class but also a teacher, a doctor, a surgeon, a lawyer, a mayor, a police officer, a governor, a business man, a landowner and a crook. Sure there are class differences, but not all Mexicans are downtrodden and solely working class. I grew up thinking Mexicans could not add or excel in the sciences, much less be a teacher, a surgeon, a lawyer or be respected for having a Mexican name with black hair. If a Los Angeles Mexican worked in a supermarket that was already success. We had no aspirations because even dreaming was too negative.

Don Memo did not comprehend that maybe these bracero offspring Mexicanoamericanos knew the limitations of White California and that survival was so tenuous, child labor was needed for survival of the family. Don Memo had been so profoundly raised in his Mexicanism that he could face the danger of the border, the migra and not be deterred while Los Angeles Mexicans are afraid to simply cross into Tijuana if they were fortunate to visit the dusty streets. The hills of Tijuana and East Los Angeles are not that different. Drive up on Gage and you will see what I mean. Don Memo was so confident in his Mexicanism that he could tell his clients to fuck off, and they would still call him because the Malibu crowd needs his construction skills, while Mexicans in Los Angeles could not really face a White confidently much less one in power. Our confidence had been stripped through the educational system and society as a whole.

I do not know what it is like to be raised in centro Mexico confidently and not worry about White people. I wish I did. I was and at times am a schizophrenic Mexican: what is normal, no se. All that I know is that I feel I am always dying but never do so because suffering is all I know, even with their pinche White titles which are a joke. If I was White, life would be different but as a Chicano male, I have to deal with bombardments of locura. Mi vida loca is plural and solitaire simultaneously.

I do not know what it is like to be a Mexican. I switch in between three identities, really four: Mexican American, Chicano, Mexican and American citizen. I have to face a damn Vietnamese Homeland Security Officer to grant my reentry and must endure his long stare; after having endured the American rejection, I face in a first class seat sitting, "Are you an American" by the White old lady with American Airlines. Even money does not remove you from the American racial caste system. Always a perpetual outsider, never belonging, but immigrant Europeans are celebrated even before they arrive: David Beckham with his tattooed neck.

Don Memo does not grasp this concept because he could be what he wanted to be, even at a young age, even if many other Mexicans like him could not. In addition, the Mexicanoamericano stigma is that we are born in the US: therefore, south of the border people do not consider us Mexicans either. I became a Mexican citizen after endless humiliations and a trip to Mexicali in the Imperial Valley because I wanted to belong but still heard from my mother say jokingly that I was an imitation Mexican. I almost cried when I was finally granted citizenship and saw the people's odd stare. My mother explained, many want to head north and you want to head south. But I solely wanted to belong to my homeland that is divided in two. Unless you are from this divide, you will not comprehend. Southern Mexicanos do not know the stigma.

Other Mexican born people do not consider us US born Mexicans Mexican. And my wife is correct when she says we do not have a Mexico to return to because our Mexico is Los Angeles. On top of both sides Mexico/US, we were already northern Mexicans on both familial sides. I do not have relatives on mainland Mexico and have not for at least fifty years; neither does my wife. My great grandmothers died in Navajoa, Sonora and Leon, Guanajuato, but that was so long ago that memories of them do not exist. I had two Mexican American sets of grandparents and one in Mexicali. Divorce explains the two. The Mexicali clan has dwindled down to almost two; my sister and tia.

South central Mexicans do not comprehend the Chicano experience, and here lies the true tragedy. Because the US has sought south central adult Mexicans, they have neglected the allure of real opportunities. And because the financial restructuring of ten dollar work days in Mexico, Mexican nationals believe the US is a land of opportunity and it is. Credit for cars is available, more pay buys more in Mexico, new credit cards are new being made available for undocumented people, but US born Mexicans have a hard time earning credit or getting stable employment with US citizenship, English and high school diplomas. Some years ago, the *Los Angeles Times* in one of their rare articles on Chicanos reported that US born Mexican American males between the ages of 18-24 had the highest unemployment rates even with the standard American report card of citizenship, high school diploma, fluent in both English and Spanish. The *Times* stated that their parents even if undocumented, no American high school education, and monolingual in Spanish were succeeding much more. I have always thought that American citizenship was relative though I am conscious of the conflict that undocumented Mexicans face. I have always been susceptible, but as my mother says, undocumented paisanos are already here and functioning so what does it matter. Even if arrested, a little visit to Mexico will not hurt and getting back is a slight inconvenience but not impossible. And us Mexican Americans get just as harassed by Border Agents; worse, they do not believe our papers are legitimate. My mother thinks that those Mexicans who visit with no papers are the most idiotic because why endanger yourself. If you wanted to move to el norte, then stay here; you know what is back there, you left for a reason, why would that change. My mother likes southern Mexicans as long as they are humble and respectful of long term Mexican Americans, but do not pretend to be better because then she hates them.

The Mexican American age 18-24 highest unemployment rate I saw in my young brother who fit that category and was utterly frustrated at the societal failure. Jorge was living the frustration of his Mexican American mother who has lived all her life from useless job to useless job. She understood though and was not harsh except when she scolded him about not completing his college education.

The tragedy in this issue was not in Mexican Americans seeking opportunities, but the reaction of White readers in the letters section a few days later. The three or four comments written by White angry people blamed the young males for having a child without a job or for purchasing an SUV. Chicanos are faithful to the American automobile industry, and the reaction by "White Niggers" is to criticize them with that Manifest Destiny hatred of 1850 California Mexicans. I bet all Mexican Americans would buy Chevrolets if given the credit opportunity. I could feel the racial hatred in their letters. White dogs, Labradors or Golden Retrievers are treated and live better than the average Mexican American. They do not have to work for White people and be despised.

Mexican nationals who have arrived in Los Angeles in the last five years do not know what it is live under racial hatred. Although they learn it quick, it might not have the same effect from being born or raised here. The *Los Angeles Times* is guilty of portraying Mexicans solely as immigrants because most of their writers come from the East Coast, so they themselves are geographical immigrants. This social construct ignorizes the primary White readership into believing Mexicans are just immigrants when more than 65% are US born; the other 25% residents are no different than most Canadians or Asians here. In all reality, the US merges US Mexicans with Mexican immigrants as immigrants only. Because we are segregated, Mexicans are always non-White and non-American. I do not have a problem because I am Mexican but US born, and I do not want this to ever change. I cannot identify with the country that invaded my country, plus Mexicans cook better than Whites. What is American food?

Media shapers including, Spanish media in the US, portray and report only on Mexicans born outside the US and never recognize the US Mexicano. When has Spanish media in the US used the word Chicano or Mexicanoamericano? They do not know what to think of us because they are also foreigners. It is much easier to conceive of Mexicans from the current border construct of Mexicans versus Mexicans from Inglewood, Lennox, Mexicali, East Los Angeles, Calexico or San Diego. Can they really exist? Can US Mexicans exist? If they knew California Mexican history, they would not succumb to the American lie of Mexicans as immigrants. But those reporters and writers see Chicanos negatively because they do not speak Spanish "correctly" or they feel they are too American. They also buy into the American immigrant myth of this is the land of opportunity, but they never bothered to ask Chicanos either US born or forty-year Mexican residents who know the truth. Long term Mexico-born Mexicans know the Mexicoamericano lies but only through time. My Nino Gus who arrived from Mexico DF-Zamora, Michoacan in 1943 was more Chicano than some of us 1970 born Mexicanoamericanos. He was my Chicano consciousness that always remained Mexicano. For him, both could coexist, and I am a product of his socialization.

My Nino Gustavo Magaña is the Chicano Patron Saint with the Pachuco picture I have of him from the 1940's. He was consciousness, and he trained me to endure the wrath of evil Whiteness by loving Mexican culture with a Chicano Apache identity. The Apaches are not dead. His view of Americans were that the Mexicans they did not like, they could easily deport but because the Mexican American is a citizen and the worst they could do to him is incarcerate him. Prisons were the deportations places for Chicanos.

The financial crisis of 1982 and 1994 by Wall Street in Mexico along with the North American Free Trade Agreement (NAFTA) did much more damage to the small business person in Mexico that the solution was to move north. This was a very logical and economical decision. The Anglos and their ever-expanding need for minimum wage brown labor were already an American institution. Therefore, we have five generations of Americans seeking Mexican labor as long as they are not American Mexicans. American Mexicans are too American for White foremen who want Mexican immigrants to work religiously and without asking for too much. Because Whites perceive Mexican Spanish-only speaking as ignorant and they do not speak Spanish either, they believe it is much easier to handle somebody who does not know their labor rights. An English speaking Mexican American is automatically viewed as lazy, but because he might know his labor rights and will not succumb to the ever lingering White American slave mentality. The ultimate spirit of the American is the perpetual need for Mexican slavery called minimum wage.

Up until the 1990's, Mexican Americans were rarely viewed as consumers because of American poverty. The George Lopez line of my car is painted in one color or only put three dollars of gas is true because I have lived it. Many times I had to decide between gas and food. Sometimes it was gas and hunger, other times hunger and limited gas while I attended college or shifted in between employment. I have probably lost more friends because they got tired of going out and me not having money to feed myself. I was embarrassed. Many times I stared at the UCLA Commons cafeteria menu and just left. A candy bar was my lunch and the Apache genes activated the insulin to save my hunger pains. I am not asking for charity, don't insult me, I want an understanding, the use of the brain to hear the Mexican American plight. I write collectively but live individualistically, this does not mean I do not hate other Chicanos, I do; you know who you are.

Mexican migrants were utilized simply because they had young strong huevos, but once you become too Americano and have aged, you'll be like an aging White model who botoxes her whole body to be perpetually young. For men, there is no hope. I hear some of my mother's male cousins mention that as men in their early fifties, they have difficulty in obtaining employment. US industries want young people and Mexican Americans are not enough because there are only 30 million of us, but Mexican nationals comprise of 105 million and counting. To earn $8 per hour versus $12 per day is a great advantage, but most will generally remain impoverished and live in barrios.

My sister is an occasional farmworker in the Imperial Valley. She lives in the eternal summer home of my mother, although my mother would never spend a summer in Mexicali. What Mexican can take a three month vacation; plus 125 degree weather is too much. My sister is one of those Mexican Americans who lives on the other side and loves the tierra. At least she is away from White people, but her kids also US Mexicans attended the wrath of Calexico schools which they completed but did not really like. As my niece Lupe stated, "The schools already had their mind made up of who would succeed and who was stupid. I was stupid, so I did not do my work." She attended continuation high school but did not complete it and is now in adult high school feeling inferior about not passing the high school exit exam. Thank you Jack Connell, State Superintendent of Education, you have with evil and contempt neglected a diploma to my niece.

My sister's experience in the field serves unexpectedly as a tool for education. Mexicali is a place where southern Mexicans either move to or move through. Mexicali, Baja California is considered the fastest growing city in the Republic of Mexico even more so than Tijuana and has the highest standard of living. The cattle fields are being swallowed up by housing developments, which are expensive. Mexicali is starting to look like a small version of Mexico D.F. I asked her if she noticed an income difference between those that work in Mexicali in the many American assembly plants or in the fields of the Imperial Valley. My sister Elizabeth replied, "Las ganacias son iguales; no hay diferencias de un lado al otro. Se gana mas en Calexico pero se gasta mas, al final viene saliendo lo mismo." The US earnings were no different than those in Mexicali. The high cost of American life resulted in the same earnings.

Elizabeth's observation was exact. According to the US 2000 Census, US Mexicans earn $9500 while the average income in Mexico is $10,000 (according to the *Los Angeles Times*). This data confirms my sister's observation that there is very little income difference between US Mexicans and Mexico Mexicans. If you want to be precise, Mexican Americans earn less than those Mexican nationals which is why some Mexican nationals who arrive to the US are not necessarily poor while many Chicanos are in the US like my family.

Some might argue that the low income earnings for Mexicans are because of their undocumented status, but if the INS cannot keep track of undocumented people because they hide in Mexican Americans neighborhoods, the US Census will have a harder time tracking them. The US Census forms are filled out by US Mexicans. This is the disturbing part, by Chicanos. At least those Mexican migrants who buy land in southern Mexico have the benefit of low property costs, but Chicanos cannot afford homes in their own country. The homeownership rates of Chicanos is the lowest of anybody; nationally Chicano homeownership does not exceed 10% as was reported in Samuel Huntington's anger book about who Americans are. Low homeownership rates do not make you an American, so his thinking is not too far off.

I heard on a Pasadena Public Radio program a commentary on assimilation and the host Larry Mantle who rubs me the wrong way stated, "I measure assimilation by homeownership." So if El Centro or East Los Angeles Chicanos never are allowed to purchase a home like my mother or three siblings, they are not Americans even if they were born here. This notion is stupid and idiotic because most Mexican Americans will never enjoy a home of their own in comparison to Whites, Asians or Blacks. I saw it in my father, and I see it in two of my brothers and now my nephew in Calexico. The American socialization is vital to understand, and yet some Mexican immigrants fail to comprehend this and are quick to judge their children.

I have heard Mexican immigrants complain:

"Why can't she get jobs besides babysitting when she has a high school diploma and speaks English?"
"Why can't he get a job?"
"Why can't he keep a job?"
"Why is he lazy?"
"Why is he not motivated?"
"Why is he taking too long to graduate from community college?"
"Why can't he get his act together at age 30?"
"It's his fault he does not want to work, not the systems?"

Add the Mexican immigrant translation and complaint of "he is not Mexican enough." He is trash, he is too American and he's a cholo, and there is deep seated conflict. Once I heard on the Superestrella 107.1 radio station: a

cultural battle take hold between Mexican immigrants and Mexicoamericanos. The Mexican immigrant stated: "The Chicanos are cultureless people,
they do not know who they are. They pretend to be Mexicans but we are the
true Mexicans". Then another person called in, a Mexicoamericana and she
stated the following:

> "Esa pendeja is mad because she does not have her papers, so they are taking it
> out that way"

The disc jockey let the discussion ensue but in reality brought forth this cultural social division that at times my friend Don Memo has for Chicanos.

And this cultural divide takes hold even in families. I was having a conversation with a young man, Roberto Mora, who lives in Whittier. His mother
was born in Los Angeles and attended high school in the area while his father
came from Mexico City as a young man. Roberto's father has this disdain for
Chicanos, and Roberto is the recipient. Roberto attends Cerritos College and
like many of us fails math because it is demanded of us when it has no practicality. Roberto got an F because he did not drop the course when he had sur-
gery and the professor kept his job by keeping him on the list even if he did
not attend class. Numbers are the sole purpose for instructional survival. Then
Roberto retook the course and got a D. When a person receives a D, that
means the instructor did not like you. If he liked you, a D could become a C
from effort. This grade has stigmatized him even though Roberto is intelligent. I should know, I was his mentor at Santa Fe Springs High School.

So Roberto is stuck in a college system where only 10-15% ever transfers
and the average transfer is 4-6 years for the equivalent of undergraduate work
for two years. Meanwhile Roberto has been out of high school for four years,
and his Mexican immigrant father begins to refer to him as lazy for not grad-
uating fast enough, and because in Mexico, he was taught much better. That
is true, the Mexican educational system teaches math much more efficiently
because they do not think of the children as stupid. Maybe cabezones but not
pendejos. Your children are not stupid, but in the US, Chicanos are not "your
children" so their education revolves around such hatred. The parents are stupid, the children are stupid, even from Mexican American teachers who majored in Liberal Studies and never received a Mexican American consciousness and who are still in identity crisis.

I asked Roberto how he deals with his father, and he told me he used to
hear him out, but that got old. I asked him what did his Chicana mother say
and he stated, "She does not get on my case as long as I am progressing but
will not say anything to him because they will get in a fight. He just does not
understand".

I recently heard from Roberto, and he wrote to me that his father and he were having more problems. Roberto had been fired from Target and was now working at Little Cesar's Pizza. That is what the Whites want from Mexicoamericanos. Dead end jobs.

This scenario is similar to Don Memo. The Mexican emigrant who does not live the American socialization of the conquered north. Mexican emigrants do not understand US Mexicans because they hold a solid Mexican regional cultural foundation. A little money in the family and they think they are better than the other neighbors. Mexicans are divided by class, and they have their occasional civil wars to mitigate such discrepancy.

The only Mexico-born Mexicans who have the mental stigma of the Chicano are those that were brought across as infants, where there is no memory of Mexico. And yet they can be the most tragic because they are socialized Americans but still undocumented. This analysis belongs to my wife. She always says that Chicanos live a tragic existence from the denial of their Apache existence to the tragedy of a piece of paper. The US can accept Chinese, Vietnamese and English immigrants, but US reared Mexicans are denied their existence even though they might be high school graduates and speak fluent English. My former guitar instructor Moises Albarran fits this description.

On the other hand, a Mexican immigrant who was given US residency might think that Ronald Reagan was great because he wanted more cheap labor but fucked previous Mexican Americans over. US Mexicans are Democrats generally but not absolutely. Mexican immigrants depending on their class and arrival date could be Republicans. That is why the merging with Cubans is not logical. The average Chicano hates the Republicans and the Cubans at the same time, plus the coconut Mexicans who pretend to be White, the Chinos and the Blacks, especially the White suburbs and puta White women.

A Mexican immigrant or a Hispanic (a closet Mexican) who likes the Republicans are enemies, and we frown upon them. My brother-in-law in Mexicali refused to continue talking to the husband of my mother's friend who was Salvadorian. Antonio would not take his calls anymore. He stated he would not be friends with somebody who was a Reagan Republican. Salvadorians, we do not like either much less when they are pro-Reagan.

My friend's husband at times I do not like because he thinks highly of Reagan because he received his residency through the 1986 Immigration Act that helped those Mexican immigrants with survival but penalized the future and assisted in their exploitation. I understand it was needed but have a broad view and think about those other Mexican Americans who were mistreated by Reagan in other ways. Even my friend states, he was raised middle class in

Ensenada (which is not saying much if they still eat tortillas as Roberto Mora stated), so he does not understand the Chicano experience. Yet he married a Chicana who says: "No East Los Angels Chicano like me would think highly of Reagan."

In essence, here is the Mexican American socialization Aztlan dual nationality divide; the US prefers Mexican immigrants, especially as adults because they serve the building effort of the White economic model and are grateful they have been given employment even if low pay and hard work.

Those Mexicans who move from pueblos in Jalisco or Michoacan feel that the US has given them more than Mexico might have because they could earn dollars, can buy a brand new car and maybe earn equity from a home purchase. While simultaneously, the US ignores Mexicoamericanos who are racially casted into barrios.

These southern Mexican emigrants are the ones who are quick to assimilate, learn English, step over other Mexicans like them all for that dollar, cry the border saga, and call their children pochos in a hateful tone. They are the ones who will think highly of the US and ignore long term Mexicoamericano frontera people who will tell you the reality. I was raised with those frontera Mexicoamericanos who would not give up their Mexican culture and are proud of being Mexicanoamericanos. That was what the Chicano was about. A proud Mexican in the US! As my friend Maricelia's mother Celia Leon who is also from Mexicali and lived in San Diego many years mentioned to me: "Yo mi cultura no la sulto, hay que defenderla hasta morir." A conscious Mexican American will defend Mexican culture until death because in the US, this is all we truly have and what White people fear the most.

Once an older White woman student told me, "Whites do not fear Mexican economic progress, it's the Mexican culture they fear the most." The fear of being culturally annihilated; economic Whites love Mexicans, for they increase their profit. The non business White fears the Mexican because of culture. And we Mexican Americans have had to endure their wrath for over a hundred and fifty years.

Maricelia's mothers comment was intended for those Mexican immigrants and Hispanics who have given up their culture for material progress. Ultimately, what material progress, to open a tortilleria? They have those in Mexico too. To dye your hair blond and hook that desperate White male and have half-breed children who are not Mexican anymore. What progress? To earn a college degree and still live in Lennox while ignoring the fact that the diploma from California State University, Dominguez Hills amounts to a niggerfied degree that is neither respected nor valued. Is UCLA Law or Medical School admitting many Cal State Los Angeles graduates?

Ultimately, the system admits those that they feel that will benefit them and Mexican immigrants, especially those special class Mexicans are loved. However, before passing, my Nino Gustavo would always state, "If it was not for Mexicoamericanos, many other Mexican nationals would not have been helped in their immigration process."

Chicanos whether through smuggling coyotes, marriage, renting out a room or work referral have helped out new arrivees even if denied. Of course competition exists, we will see if universities or the movie industry will help out in Mexico City. Nonetheless, once Mexicoamericanos get to know you, they will help to the best of their ability. Even Salvadorians have benefited from unfortunately marrying Mexicans. If not for the Mexican coyotes in Mexicali or Sonora, more Salvadorians would have died or not received their residency. Give us credit.

However, in the process of admission into Americana, the Chicano has been left out. The statistics tell the story, but even then, Chicanos are not bashing southern Mexicans though I know some do. Mexicoamericanos have generally welcomed Mexicans and adopted them because more Mexicans throw off the White discourse and reinforces Mexican Chicano culture. It is better to have more Mexicanos than Centro Americans, Armenians or Chinos. I believe the US allows other people in because they do not want the sole blood influence of Mexicans to dominate, which is why they intentionally categorize us a White ethnic group versus a race. Everybody knows Mexicans are a race which is why academic Anglophiles such as Victor Hanson and Samuel Huntington cry about the racial dominance of Mexicans. But they are really crying about too many Mexicas born here. Isn't the word Victor Mexican? Even so- called Native Americans complain about Mexicans. How can they be native if they are white—half does not count— and reject maiz based people from the desert?

In actuality, the average Mexican does not want to move to the US. They have 106 million people in Mexico, if 10 million decide to move at one time, Homeland Security would not know what to do with them. The average Mexican stays in Mexico.

The majority is wanted for agricultural and other manual labor, but as I earlier stated, professionals do come. The small group that wants access to Hollywood are not related to Chicanos; does Salma Hayek know what a Chicano is? She definitely does not want one; se coje the United Nations but not a local Mexicoamericano.

The Hollywood arts crowd is open to some Polanco or Condesa El Colegio de Mexico snob but not to the Apache looking Mexicans from Los Angeles. And here begins the complex nature of Americana, because they want to showcase the Mexican immigrants who arrived with no papers and later opened a tire rim store or earned a PhD in education. They use them as the Mexican success story while the second or third generation struggles to get into graduate school. I belong to that category; do not engage in self hate but somebody has to challenge this myopic view.

In conversations with us Mexicoamericano and Mexicans, I have realized many of us are quietly carrying a burden of what we feel is unfair. In the trade arts, Chicanos are viewed as lazy and not hardworking. Whites want to be able to have the opportunity to exploit and return you to Mexico if you misbehave, but the US Mexican is left out. My friend Ruben states: "Immigrant Mexicans are given better access because they want to exploit them, but it still means progress for them while I do not have a car at age 33. I am not going to critique because it seems that even ex prison convicts have more opportunities. But more Mexicans help us out by mere presence."

Yet it is in professional circles that this becomes more apparent. I have seen that a Mexico-born educated in the US person fits their model of American opportunity very similar to the Chicana who is admitted into the PhD program while a male is left out. The Mexican immigrant model of we crossed the border, we were undocumented, we made it with no papers serves as the typical American dream model until you see the next generation or the Mexican American struggling with math because they have made him feel all his life that he is inferior. Or he cannot pass the math section of the state examination for graduate school, scores low on the graduate entrance exam and lives day to day even with White titles from UCLA and USC. The rules do not apply the same to Mexican Americans.

When I was at UCLA in graduate school, I talked to a guy named Octavio Pescador who was an undergraduate. His father was the Mexican consulate in Los Angeles, former mayor of Mazatlan, former minister of education under Ernesto Zedillo and his son attended UCLA while the average Chicano from Los Angeles had never set foot on the White campus. How did he know what the Chicano experience was like?

Quite frequently when I watch the chisme news on Univision, I see Octavio Pescador provide opinion on Mexican and US topics as he now runs the Paulo Friere Center at UCLA. Who has been given access and who has not? Prior to that, he taught adjunct at Cal State Los Angeles in Chicano Studies and had no idea what Chicano Culture was. He taught because of his name and not knowledge while a Chicano like me could have taught that subject. Even back in the class we took together, the Mexico City- born professor at UCLA Raul Hinojosa told Octavio he was not the average Mexican and much less the average Los Angeles Mexican American because even this instructor was not.

There is a disdain for Los Angeles Mexicans. We are the vermin and cholo as one, but the fresa Mexicano del DF is loved. At California State University, Long Beach, the Harvard education specialist that I like a lot, enough to write him a letter of recommendation for his tenure, Jose Moreno is more apologetic and somewhat resentful to fellow Chicanos who picked on him because he was not a US citizen. Granted there are culeros on both sides, because I still deal with the Pocho syndrome and not Mexican because I was born eight miles from the border but in the same ecological zone. Yet, I feel he is more apologetic and too Latino, not protective enough of Chicano Studies. The Harvard paradigm has taught him to be Latino and hesitant of being too nationalistic, so he is open to non-Mexicans teaching Chicano Studies which is poisonous. Did he get hired because of the Harvard degree and the status Chicano Studies needed because before his arrival, the elder Luis Arroyo once told me that an EdD would not be enough to be hired in the department, but when it is from Harvard, all rules are bent?

Even Cal State Los Angeles has a Salvadorian-born Esther Hernandez teaching Chicano Studies. What does a Salvadorian know about Los Angeles Mexicans? Different nationalities, different cultures, different geographies and different people entirely! UC Irvine has a known unspoken racial rule of keep the Mexicans out. What do the universities know about Mexicans? How to collect data? Data is not culture. And much less from an outsider we do not like. Let us see if Chicanos would be allowed to teach "Salvadorians Studies." The same exists at UC Santa Barbara with Horacio Roque. I was enrolled in a class with him in Portuguese at UCLA; he is not Chicano, not by blood or birth. How is this possible? But to not exclude Tara Yosso and Ralph Armbruster, two Whites? Why have Chicano Studies? What an insult and blasphemy. Part of Mexican American studies should be the Mexican American experience as the program literature at University of Texas, Austin states. How can a person teach Chicano Studies if the experience does not accompany the academic? Ask women if men can teach about a woman's period or birth. They will laugh and yet for Chicanos, we are all meshed without taking into account the history of Los Angeles Mexicans.

It is not solely Latinos-non Mexicans but also southern born Mexicans who are favored such as the Manual Bravos; Carlos Fuentes; Ricardo Legorretas; Frida Kahlos; Diego Riveras; Carlos Monsivais; Hugo Sanchez; Luis Mandokis and Ilan Stavans.

Even in conversation with the ever philosopher friend of mine, Marcos Ramos, who works as an undergraduate advisor at Berkeley, Marcos stated that his girlfriend who was born and spent early educational years in Parral, Chihuahua was able to get into graduate school with a lower GPA than his. His previous previous novia, was born in Oaxaca and in one immigrant generation had been given access. A couple of ex-girlfriends of mine, one from Michoacan, the other Colima and a Bolivian were all able to obtain higher educational degrees while my Mexican American mother and father were not. The one from Colima hated the Chicano slang and eventually I came to hate her for that. So what if we are Cholos, it is not as if we decided to become Xolos. For some, Cholos also means low class. Come on, her old man was a bracero. The Sahuayo woman was raised from an earlier age in Wilmington, but she was quick to add the White feminism and preferred non Mexican males. I came to hate her too; I was happy she left me. As my Nino Gus stated, "Viejas sobran a monton." Don Memo stated, "Mujeres se acercan como moscas. Women get near like flies."

If we throw in the Tejano Paradigm of the lower Rio Grande Valley, then the Chicano-Califorence is really excluded? The Califorence Mexicano does not exist.

Marcos feels that the sympathy story at Berkeley always excludes the Chicano and gives preference to people born in other parts of the world but might have come from the son of a National Guard Officer during the Somoza Dictatorship in Nicaragua or a Right Wing Vietnamese. Why should Asian or Centro American foreigners with no history to northern Mexico be included? Is this not the Black argument about Barack Obama, he does not have the Black experience?

Chicanos should be given preferential treatment because they are native to lands conquered by the Americans, Central Americans or Vietnamese are not? The same applies to Mexican immigrants because the person who comes as an adult and survives employment has succeeded, the person who wants to earn some money and returns has met his goal but what about the Chicano even if Mexico-born but has no memory? Where does he reside? Especially for the majority of second or third generation Mexican Americans because we seem to be stuck while globalization takes hold. Let the world exploit us.

My generation does not even have the Chicano feel good era. And as I was once told by James Diego Vigil at USC in 1990: "In 1970, there was a lot of money for higher education, not today." And today is when I need it the most and so does my cuate Ruben, mi carnal Alberto y Jorge; my uncle Ronnie; my nephew Tony; my niece Lupita and my neighbor Bobby who still drives a twenty-year old Toyota Four Runner.

Where does the Los Angeles Mexican exist? Does he exist?

I see that he does not subsist. In Spanish media, he is dead whether it is television or radio. As somebody told me, Jorge Ramos looks exactly like Anderson Cooper. On Spanish radio, the stations on ranchera or banda music are dominated by people born in Mexico. Piolin is showcased in the *Los Angeles Times West Magazine* as an influential person who snuck across in the trunk of a car but is now a success story.

Even Centro Americans like El Cucuy Renan Coelho and he is one feo looking dude can be the host of ranchera music but a Chicano cannot. Piolin has a Salvadorian co-host. That damn accent cannot be more repulsing. How about a Cholo co-host?

A few Chicanas can be admitted, but she has cleavage and have you heard her and the male host on KLVE. They could not be any worse. Even the Super Estrella station has a Peruvian and Chilango but no Chicano. Chicanos love rock en español. Right now as I write, I was called from the Mana concert from my two Chicana friends Maricelia Carmona and Ana Leon: "Como quisieria poder vivir sin aire, pero no puedo, siento que muero, me estoy ahogando." But maybe not, Cheech is right, Mexican Americans do not like to get up too early.

Mexican Americans are entirely ignored. In these ranchera-norteña stations, they never play Los Lobos; Freddy Fender; Flaco Jimenez and their great songs are the ones in Spanish. Los Lobos are liked for their Cholo blues, but most of us want to see ourselves play those songs. And I mean ourselves as Mexican Americans singing to Volver Volver, Sabor A Mi, Carabina 30-30 or Las fiestas de las flores. Even La Bamba, as the Richie Valens character stated: "If Nat King Cole can sing in Spanish, why can't I."

My wife a Huntington Beach Chicana Guera who grew up speaking English only loves Los Lobos for their Mexican folklore. So we must be able to express ourselves. My mother loves Lupillo Rivera because he represents Los Angeles Mexicans, a ranchero xolo who is now pelon, but she loves his style for he is from these sacred lands of the Chicano Apache. He must have his cultural space and yet he does not.

Even in writing, the Mexican American is loathed. At the Libreria Martinez in Santa Ana, Ruben Martinez mentioned to me that the Spanish reading audience does not want anything to do with the selection of Chicano books. Damn, maybe we are aliens, foreign to the US, foreign to Mexico, lodged into permanent purgatory.

In essence that is why I take on my Apache Mexican identity more than solely the Mexican. For me, they are the same, but why tell people I am Mexican, they do not believe me. When I tell them I am Apache they do, whether in el DF or Los Angeles. At least in el DF I am a curiosity because I am tall and I speak Mexican Spanish clearly and I am proud of being both Mexicano, Chicano, Mexican American. In Los Angeles I am just loco. I live in a foolish, wild and indifferent society. I am from the north and I love futbol de la liga Mexicana, I just don't have a favorite team because I do not come from any of those spaces.

In 2004, we traveled to Veracruz, Veracruz. I fell in love with that place. There are no Blacks in Veracruz, just Totonaco people, Jarochos. Great food, puros y Jarochas que no se la acaba uno.

After visiting the Spanish fort from where they looted Mexico, we took a taxi in the scorching sun. When we got in and the man introduced himself, he looked like George Lopez's father. Ramon was his name. As we got to know each other, he asked where were we from? When I mentioned, Los Angeles, he yelled in emotion, "I lived there once many years ago." He showed me his laminated driver's license from California, and he began to ask me: "Tell me about the Cholos, do they cruise along Whittier Blvd. with their lowriders, nicely dressed up with their firme style?" I felt he was stuck in *Boulevard Nights,* but he told me something about the 1970's Los Angeles that he had lived as a young man.

He then asked me if it was true that the Chinese had taken over the swap-meets because in the 1970's it was primarily Mexicans and then I thought, you are right. Don Monchis was a Chicano from Mexicali who had relocated to southern Mexico and to forget about the north. He had obtained some money through contraband, hey Whites need their fix, he was just responding to their market demand. He was a good capitalist, but Don Monchis who was from the Nacozari colonia in Mexicali needed to obliterate el norte.

As he later told me, what are the undocumented jobs? They are not worth anything.

He even had the Cholo strut and dress as was visible in his pants. He still had his norteño accent because the Jarochos were hard to comprehend. When he asked me if he could play Chalino Sanchez, I was in heaven. Here we were these norteños way south in the gulf of Mexico with real crab I did not like and brujas who were trying to make a buck but were scared when they saw me. He would state, "Al jarocho no les gustan las norteñas (musica) y son mas flojos que la chingada. Mira, aqui no hay tanta pobreza como en Mexicali. Aqui siembran palos y nacen arboles sin hacer nada. El Jarocho es flojo y no trabajador como el Cachanilla. El del norte saber trabajar."

Don Monchis made me laugh so much because he would say, "The Jarocho (Veracruz native) does not like northern Mexican music and they are lazy as hell. In Veracruz you don't see poverty like in Mexicali. Here a planted stick will grow into a tree with little effort. The Veracruzano is lazy and is not a worker like someone from Mexicali. The people from the north know how to work."

I just laughed. In the north, the southerners tell Chicanos they are lazy, in the south the northerners say we are hardworkers. I thought, maybe he is George Lopez's father, he was too comical.

Later, on a boat trip to Catemaco where they filmed a Sean Connery flick, I hit my head and my natural outburst was: "Chingada madre, ay cabron, chingada madre, hijos de su chingada madre."

When all of a sudden Don Monchis laughed and stated: "Si es Mexicano, si es Mexicano con ese vocabulario. He is Mexican with his vocabulary, he is Mexican.

Chapter Ten

Higher Education As Ignorance

"Look, if we don't know it already, chances are we are not interested in learning it."

The Milagro Beanfield War

One of my favorite films is titled "The Milagro Beanfield War." This film is based on a book by the same name from John Nichols. Based in Nuevo Mexico, this story deals with the land struggle Mexicans encounter as Whites move in; soon new laws are incorporated that favor Whites from issues of land to water and the hardship Mexicanos live under American rule. To even pushing legislation to ban cockfighting! Fucken New Yorkers!

I love this film. The casas de adobe, the dirt roads, the junky cars, the cynicism, the belief in santos y animas, fiado, the outhouses, the cochise, the chisme, the lowriders with their bandanas, the pisto, the tractor, los cohetes, the terregal-dust in the air from the vehicles, the vacas, the reference to the Treaty of Guadalupe Hidalgo, the name Lupita, clotheslines, the gas tank connected to the house, the porches, the ramadas, the small canales, the use of Spanish, the Chicano accent, the cross on the wall, the Chevy pick up trucks, the wandering chickens, la cantina, the tortilla maker, the abarrotes as a hang out place with bottled coca cola and gansitos, the bandanas with the lokes look and the sombreros.

I see my family, myself in this film. I see the purity and the infighting at once, but most of all I see a Mexico that slowly has dwindled away. This Inglewood Mexican rancho is now dead and even in Mexicali, the rancho is not the same anymore.

The Rancho Roa died twenty five years ago, but the newer rancho is now called a colonia and even that beauty has become more urbanized where wheat chamizo fields no longer abound, but large trailer parks do. In the early 1980's, corral wooden fences were enough with barb wire to mark personal property demarcations, but today the divide is based on chain link fences. Before, even with the barb wires, the neighboring dogs could visit and that included the canines, yet today these divisions are becoming permanent because of the unknown strangers. No more milking cows, no more crossing through the chamizo fields. Now chemical factories intoxicate the colonia, chain link gates guard the night and the gallinero awaits its final cleansing.

The chicken coop is soon to meet its own funeral. My sister wants to cremate the ancient wooden structure where chickens once fed us organically during our visits from Los Angeles where we traveled back in time within California. So extreme and so complex to understand the beauty, it has taken me thirty years to begin the sacred search. And when I began to, it was time for my ama and apa to be returned to the sagrada tierra Mother Earth. They had to replenish the earth with their bodies, and my sister wants to ash the earth and rest this past. If not for my brother-in-law wanting to preserve the gallinero, it would have already gone up in smoke. I am torn, what good is a gallinero, with no chickens, but once gone, my ama Alberta will be entirely released.

The rancho is our church; our Mexican Apache church, and we want to preserve it as much as possible even to the point of becoming a Mexican citizen to do so. I want to preserve my culture and heritage in Mexican California.

When I first saw *The Milagro Beanfield War*, I was amazed to see myself in those images. The ranchos of Mexicali are not that different from the ranchos in northern New Mexico. My mother can attest to that. When she saw an Ansel Adams picture of Hernandez, New Mexico with the Luna Rising, she stated, "Mira, alli esta Mexicali. Casas de adobe, plano y rodeado con las montañas." She was right, you cannot tell the difference from Baja California to New Mexico. I am not one to celebrate any aspect of White culture, but to have an image of a similar rancho was hard to ignore. Psychologically and spiritually, I am a ranchero at heart. I long for the rancho that was taken from me in Inglewood (I at least enjoyed it as a child when work and school did not matter).

Yet the part of this film that captures me the most is when a White graduate student arrives with his East Coast credentials to study what he calls southwest cultures. As he gets off the bus with his books and typewriter, already he is out of place. He is out of place simply by being in that pueblo, and everybody knows who he is: an outsider.

The graduate student approaches Mayor Cantu performed by the original Chicano Tejano musico: Freddy Fender. Freddy was singing norteñas in both Spanish and English three decades before it was popular. Que descanse en paz!

The following takes place:

"Herbie Platt department of Sociology, NYU." (He points to his chest.) "I'm writing a thesis, I have a grant to do research."

The New Mexican mayor from the pueblo looks at him with amazement and bewilderment, not comprehending his references to NYU very similar to my sister not understanding why a US born Mexican would be enrolled at Berkeley studying English if she was already from the US.

The mayor was not impressed by the references to New York University, and after more frustrating dialogue and references about teaching children, the alcalde responds, "Look, if we don't know it already, chances are we are not interested in learning it."

Later, the White graduate student is given shelter in an adobe structure and put to work in a bean field like a regular Mexican, picking frijoles-beans.

The comment, "Look, if we don't know it already, chances are we are not interested in learning it," resonates heavily in me. I view this comment as Mexicans being portrayed as uneducated but with truth. What can the university teach the rancho? Mexican ranchos have been around longer than any American university.

Can the university teach the rancho how to make adobe bricks? An adobe house? Mexicano-Chicano architecture? Mexican food? Chile? Maiz? Tortillas? Does the university have a class on how to make tortillas, how to farm Mexican products such as tomatoes, lettuce, frijoles? How to learn Mexican Spanish? Champurrado, carnitas, enchiladas, wienes con huevos? How to divert water through canales con palas-shovels? How to use an asadon? How to make sombreros? How to make tacos or tamales? Do they know about animas, limpias, un vaso de agua and mal de ojo? Do they know the property elements of ruda, yerba buena, marihuana, peyote, cilantro and oregano? Do they have classes on how to make menudo and pozole in higher education? Café de olla? Could they teach the arts of tejer and cobija making from left over clothing or flour sacks? Could they teach you how to sing in Mexican? Make references to the paloma, el sauce y la palma, hermosisimo lucero y la llorona. Could they teach Mexicans about the tambora, Banda Sinaloence or el accordeon estilo Ramon Ayala con sus tragos de amargo licor? Cumbias and mariachis classes and how to dance cholo style? Would they teach a course on Chalino Sanchez and his influence on corridos? Las Jilguerillas.

How about how to raise a chicken and then break its neck with bare hands and machete the head off, pluck the feathers and make caldo de pollo, fresh? Do universities know how to make carnitas, mole or chiles rellenos Julian Camacho style?

Do universities teach us to conserve our culture? Do they teach us to preserve our names, our language, and the oral traditions? Do any American schools teach Chicanos to feel proud and be themselves? Do they admit many Chicanos beyond the 10% cut off brown line?

I have noticed that those who have attended college in my mother's generation tend to act more White and disdain Mexican culture while those like my parents who did not attend college are more proud to be Mexicans. They speak Spanish, love norteñas, eat chile, act Mexicano and do not pretend to be something they are not. And they are educated just not in the "Humanities" definition. What good does knowledge of European art and Roman civilization do for people who come from ranchos in California? Will those classes teach them how to work the soil and make picadillo and coktel de camarones?

My grandfather Gus taught me to comprehend racial America because as he stated, "A un mexicano nunca lo van a dejar subir." A Mexican would never be allowed to advance. Hence thirty years before critical race theory made headways, my grandfather was educating me orally about the future. Was he ever correct, because in my undergraduate, high school and even graduate education, American racism was ignored intentionally while society was being judged by race. And the minor focus was on Blacks as if they were in their native lands. Are you going to tell a Chicano Apache that he does not belong in Los Angeles? And yet they did.

My Nino Gus taught me to value myself, Mexican traditions, to be critical of irony, to love Mexico with all its deformities as one loves their barrio. He taught me to listen, to be a friend, to defend myself, to not be manipulated by women, to wear a sombrero, to never forget where we come from because to be Apache is eternal. He was my philosopher who taught me what I needed to learn for the journey of aging.

In essence, even he comprehended that I have it harder. He only had to Mexicanize brown gringos. I have to Mexicanize mixed Whites which I am not sure will be possible, but I know I must try nonetheless.

Long before scientific studies, Mexican culture taught us what we need to know to live. My mother taught me the following:

A good diet will keep you healthy. Frijoles, chiles, zanahorias, maiz, arroz is all vital to living.

Ear aches are cured by hot olive oil in cotton with ruda in the ear.

Manzanilla tea cures stomach ailments and eye irritations.

Being overweight is healthier than being underweight. Mexican culture has always associated being gordo as the good life. When I see a thin person, I sense he is not healthy. When my primo was size 48, he might have been gordito, but he was healthy. When AIDS consumed him, his loss of weight meant his death was approaching. He died at size 28, I believe even his head shrunk.

After his death, my mother mentioned to me that she remembered my grandmother's younger brother, a doctor out in the ejidos advised my tia in the mid 1970's that my cousin needed testosterone shots. Another cousin also needed them and received them while Antonio did not. My mother wondered if his death could have been avoided.

And recently, more evidence pinpoints that the increase in testosterone can make one more male and not feminine. It is a hormonal imbalance, and yet my mother's uncle himself a man of Mexican science was more ahead than any American doctor. But because he is Mexican, he is inferior even if educated.

My apa Matiaz would always say that dogs could cure with their saliva and that they were more intelligent and could speak. Was he ever correct? Now it turns out that dogs have penicillin in their saliva and have the ability to detect cancer through their scent of smell. When my Cholosizquintlis Tixoc or Simon smell other cacas, they are detecting characteristics no different than when a doctor collects stool samples. Caca is medicine.

Even the ability of canines to see through the dark demonstrates the power of animals beyond a comprehension we humans have. The more Mexicans are Anglocized, the more detached we become from nature.

Linguistically speaking, my dogs are bilingual. They understand when I speak to them in Spanish and English. What is a White person's excuse for not learning Mexican Spanish? And I have learned to speak my dog's language too. Their bark tones let you know something is going on, apart from their awareness of danger. My beautiful Simon once saw his son Cahua almost fall off the sofa, so he ran across the living room and bumped him up. He prevented the puppy from getting hurt where I could not. The power of the dogs. I believe Mexicans originate from the Mexican canine. For nature reasons, we became upright but we have not allowed ourselves to be separated from them and them from us. The lobo, coyote, chihuahua are all manifestations of us. Mexican dogs even look like us.

When I traveled to Holland in 2006, I was surprised to see how ugly the dogs were, but then again the people were not very attractive and both species looked very similar. One reason why Dutch men marry out in high numbers especially in Los Angeles to Mexican women is because they do not really have many choices at home and they want to better the blood. These are the only "Whites" Mexicans really marry because the Hollanders did not comprehend the social racial rules; they just saw pretty women and the ideal of Mexican food inspired them. You should have seen my father-in-law with his Mexican taste buds. He loved his deep fried Apache tacos.

Another piece of cultural knowledge gone "scientific" is Marihuana. This cultural plant that Mexicans sing to and have smoked from the Aztec era has proven to be medically useful. All Mexican abuelas had their marihuana in a bottle of alcohol used to oint for arthritis or joint pains. Miama Alberta used to store it in the closet secretively, but we could always see it. Now that Whites need the remedy properties of marihuana, they have begun to challenge its illegality, but when Mexicans stated it was medicinal, they would be arrested and prosecuted. I have written a few letters to judges asking them to not incarcerate Chicanos for smoking this natural unprocessed leaf. If it is Willie Nelson; it is in style; when Julian Camacho smokes it, it is a crime.

Mexicans have always known that marihuana was used to counter cataracts, but in American eyes, inferior people could not educate the superior race. The marihuana helps me with my vision problems. I can see better. The criminalization of marihuana has intentionally led to the high increase of alcoholism because before the yesca allowed, a man to relax from a long day of work. He is now doing more labor intensive slave work and the only way he can relief the effects is by purchasing cerveza which is more addictive and hardful versus a marihuana cigarette. Some men have been forced to turn to heavier narcotics such as cocaine or methamphetamines to endure long hours of field work or construction.

The question begged in this body of work is to query the value of American higher education versus Mexican cultural education, and at no level does American schooling supersede rancho knowledge.

My mother was educated in four fields from her upbringing that have helped her survive, and yet her knowledge has always been considered inferior because of her race. What good is an essay on literary criticism, which most cannot comprehend versus the art of Mexican cooking, sewing, yerbas, singing and rearing five healthy males in the height of the Reagan onslaught. In addition to learning White rules that benefit whites only.

Higher education for Mexicans is ignorance. We arrive at the university speaking two languages and leave not feeling good about ourselves. We leave with self doubt, embarrassed about pronouncing our names correctly, and the most harmful, questioning our parents' native knowledge which is more ancient and in tune with the earth than any Shakespeare play or Catholic mass or American history book. Chalino Sanchez, Ramon Ayala, Mana and Jaguares make Mexican American youth feel much better about themselves than any White school.

Even American history is pendejo, more propaganda than accuracy. Or geographically wrong. White writers cannot even get the culture correct in California. Many will use the term Hispanic when no Mexican uses that term to refer to his culture and much less desert Apachis or Zunis. And they believe they are smarter.

Personally speaking, I was rejected from three or four academic PhD programs, but in the long run, I am glad I was because I have been able to write my ideas out without anybody telling me I am right or wrong. Read an academician's writing, and see how they cannot write. Plus, their attitudes of playing like God attempting to predict some theory most get wrong. Nobody can predict the future, and yet they act like they can. Most White studies of Mexicans have always been proven wrong so data collection does not provide one with insight into the cultural psycho realm. Only living the culture does.

Because of the incorruption of my mind and really the continued segregation of me both by White and Chicano academies, I have been able to write with my own visions and ideals based on culture. The validation of Mexican culture. Since I was a child, I was told by the clan that I would write not in White terms, but in Mexican oral terms. All I had to do was listen and open my eyes. Chicano Mexicano Apache cultural, is powerful and I am barely beginning to scrape the surface that only through time will be possible: the good and the bad.

I have had four books published without White counsel, solely by listening. As my mother taught me from my early interactions with her, "Escucha mijo, piensa, siempre piensa," Always think!

1977, Kenwood Street, Inglewood

My Nino Gus was the person who would take my brother Alberto to kindergarten at 11 am because my father and mother were at work. My Nino having retired helped us out through the ever-demanding removal of the mother from the household.

My father and Nino Gus would sit around and play barajas, poker. They would sit for hours and learn the cycles of cards and numbers that I have never cared for. Too much math for me. Alberto was always there with my father. I followed my Nina Kika and ama Monica more. I was more attached to the women, but I was an admirer of the men.

Because Alberto was always with my father Julian, he learned to enjoy his activities.

Therefore, on this one occasion and I heard it from my Nino who was a fantastic story teller. He gave the moment life where we all laughed. And he did not let us down.

He began by telling us that he had played cards alone with Alberto sitting at the table with him, and when time neared for him to taking him to kindergarten, Mi Nino Gus got ready by putting on his sombrero and jacket and told Alberto he was going to take him to school.

My brother Alberto is ocurrente, original, a straight forward character. When my Nino told him he was going to drop him off at Oak Street Elementary, Alberto's five year old response was , "No, porque mejor no me quedo a jugar barajas con usted. No, I would rather stay and play cards with you."

My Nino told us, he scolded and told him; "No, your mother is expecting me to take to you school." "No Nino, I would rather stay and play cards with you."

I remember my Nino telling us the story and feeling guilty about his light scold, but then laughing and feeling a sense of pride because barajas was something the two fathers played. The five year old was only imitating the abuelo as he laughed at his honesty.

Nino felt guilty for teaching him bad habits, but he was teaching him how to think and to count.

Montebello 2002:

My friend Rosalinda Moctezuma's mother-in-law died; the sad and tense air permeated their house. After a couple months of not seeing them after the funeral, on a visit, I gave Adrian and Miguel my condolences. I asked Miguel how was he handling her death and his response was profound:

"My mother taught me everything I needed to learn for life."